STORIES OF WOMEN IN THE MIDDLE AGES

Maria Teresa Brolis

STORIES *of* WOMEN
in the MIDDLE AGES

FOREWORDS BY FRANCO CARDINI
AND GILES CONSTABLE

Translated by Joyce Myerson

McGill-Queen's University Press
Montreal & Kingston · London · Chicago

© McGill-Queen's University Press 2018
Originally published in 2016 as *Storie di donne nel Medioevo* by Società editrice il Mulino, Bologna

ISBN 978-0-7735-5478-8 (cloth)
ISBN 978-0-7735-5479-5 (paper)
ISBN 978-0-7735-5614-0 (ePDF)
ISBN 978-0-7735-5615-7 (ePUB)

Legal deposit fourth quarter 2018
Bibliothèque nationale du Québec

Printed in Canada on acid-free paper that is 100% ancient forest free (100% post-consumer recycled), processed chlorine free

The translation of this work has been funded by SEPS
Segretariato Europeo per le Pubblicazioni Scientifiche
Via Val d'Aposa 7 –
40123 Bologna – Italy
seps@seps.it – www.seps.it

Funded by the Government of Canada   Financé par le gouvernement du Canada   Canadä

Canada Council for the Arts   Conseil des arts du Canada

We acknowledge the support of the Canada Council for the Arts, which last year invested $153 million to bring the arts to Canadians throughout the country.

Nous remercions le Conseil des arts du Canada de son soutien. L'an dernier, le Conseil a investi 153 millions de dollars pour mettre de l'art dans la vie des Canadiennes et des Canadiens de tout le pays.

Library and Archives Canada Cataloguing in Publication

Brolis, Maria Teresa, 1959–
[Storie di donne nel Medioevo. English]
Stories of women in the Middle Ages / Maria Teresa Brolis ; forewords by Franco Cardini and Giles Constable ; translated by Joyce Myerson.

Translation of: Storie di donne nel Medioevo.
Includes bibliographical references.
Issued in print and electronic formats.
ISBN 978-0-7735-5478-8 (cloth). –
ISBN 978-0-7735-5479-5 (paper). –
ISBN 978-0-7735-5614-0 (ePDF). –
ISBN 978-0-7735-5615-7 (ePUB)

1. Women – Europe – Biography.
2. Women – History – Middle Ages, 500–1500.   I. Title.   II. Title: Storie di donne nel Medioevo. English.

D109.B7613 2018
920.72
C2018-904225-7

C2018-904226-5

Set in 11.5/14.5 Mrs Eaves OT with Agedage SimpleVersal
Book design & typesetting by Garet Markvoort, zijn digital

FOR FRANCO

along with Attilio and Marco

CONTENTS

PART TWO: ORDINARY WOMEN

FOREWORD TO THE ENGLISH EDITION

This book introduces the reader to a group of sixteen medieval women, of whom eight are well-known and eight are described here as "ordinary" in the sense of unremarkable. Together they throw light on many aspects of life in the Middle Ages that are relatively unknown as compared with the lives or activities of men. The famous women are Hildegard of Bingen, who is known as an abbess, writer, and musician; Raingarde, the mother of Peter the Venerable and other influential churchmen of the twelfth century; Heloise, the pupil (and lover) of Abelard and subsequently abbess of the Paraclete; Eleanor of Aquitaine, the wife of King Louis VII of France and King Henry II of England and the mother of several other kings; Clare, the founder of the mendicant house of St Damian at Assisi; Bridget of Sweden, the mystic and visionary and founder of the Bridgetine order; Christine of Pizan, whose writings are a valuable source for the intellectual and social history of the late Middle Ages; and Joan of Arc, who is labelled here a rebel.

The eight "ordinary" women came from the region of Bergamo, an important centre of economic and religious activity, on which the author's research has concentrated. They are mostly of lower social status than the "famous" group and are sometimes described by historians as invisible because little is known about them, especially their private lives. Here they are identified by their names and by what the author calls their "small stories" illustrating their occupations and activities. Most of them were poor, but a few were quite prosperous and ran successful businesses.

They are identified in the titles with business (Flora), poverty (Agnesina), marriage (Ottebona), religious life (Grazia), fashion (Gigliola), potions (Bettina), care-giving (Margherita), and the road, that is, travel and pilgrimage (Belfiore).

There are many parallels and overlaps between these women, though they came from very different social and economic backgrounds. The importance of religion and religious life is striking. Hildegard, Heloise, Clare, and Grazia were all the founders or heads of religious houses; Bridget and Clare both founded religious orders; Bridget and Belfiore were pilgrims; others spent time as hermits or recluses. The so-called "ordinary" women, perhaps owing to the nature of the sources, were more concerned than the "famous" women with practical matters of health, care-giving, and clothing, and their lives, as recorded here, give an idea of the everyday occupations of women. Their stories challenge in many respects the conventional assumptions about medieval women and show that they played a considerable part in religious as well as secular life, serving among other things as preachers and scribes. "The theme of aid volunteered by women in diverse ways and places," the author writes, "in the home and in the hospital, deserves its very own discussion ... because it represented one of the most penetrating and powerful aspects, although often a hidden one, of female presence not only in the medieval period, but throughout history."

Many questions that are frequently overlooked or insufficiently studied are thus opened up by this book. "Can an historian enter into the house of a medieval woman," the author asks, "not only to peek at her furniture and clothes ... but also to uncover behaviours and even the feelings of individuals?" She especially emphasizes that the theme of heresy needs to be re-examined "in the light of the most recent historiography" and that "the presumed or real heterodox inclination often attributed to Bergamesque citizens ... is configured more as a political alignment than as an actual deeply rooted religious choice." The answers to these and other questions about medieval women, as this book shows, are often yes, though not without limitations. *Stories of Women in the Middle Ages* opens the door to further wide-ranging research into many questions that need to be studied.

Giles Constable

FOREWORD TO THE ITALIAN EDITION

In comparison to modern or contemporary studies, European medieval studies have been less touched by issues related to gender. Particular themes associated with philosophy have elicited some interest – and we acknowledge here the beautiful writing by Michela Pereira dedicated to the theme *Né Eva, né Maria* (Neither Eve nor Mary) – as have those studies specifically oriented towards memoir or epistolography, albeit in very different contexts, between Heloise and Alessandra Macinghi Strozzi. In this regard, the by now "classic" work by Georges Duby, introduced in the relatively distant past, has achieved great significance in framing the issue. In the context of synthesis, we have the propitious work by Edith Ennen, dedicated to women in the Middle Ages, that is about thirty or forty years old. Eight more recent "exemplary" (in the etymological sense of the word) essays were written thanks to the collaboration between Maria Teresa Beonio Brocchieri Fumagalli, Ferruccio Bertini, and Claudio Leonardi, and issued by the publisher Laterza in 2001, with the title *Medioevo al femminile* (*The Middle Ages from a Female Perspective*). These are all works boasting extensive longevity.

Of course, a kind of unresolved ambiguity lies at the root of this "historiographic genre." Are we faced with "cases," in which randomness rules when they are being chosen, or with "models," presupposing a certain seriality in terms of tactics and heuristic and methodological strategies?

The rigorous taxonomy applied by Maria Teresa Brolis must not deceive us, nor, more importantly, reassure us. The dividing line indeed seems rather clear: eight famous women in the first part, eight "ordinary" women in the second. There is no doubt that, in terms of fame, the author flies high and demonstrates courage: over a time frame spanning the twelfth to the fifteenth centuries inclusively, eight great protagonists parade before us, from the decisive centuries of the history of Western and World Christianity, dealing with the definitely golden decades that stretch between the era of Bernard de Clairvaux and that of Francis of Assisi – the great European spring! – the years which Maria Teresa obviously favours, and to which she dedicates five distinct profiles (a theological/philosophical and maybe even magical genius, a mother to whom destiny dealt the task of bringing into the world a true demiurge of the twelfth century, a bold and ardent love-struck woman, a duchess who twice became a queen, and a founder of a religious Order who, in the name of love for Christ, rejected any ambiguity which could have relegated her to a role of subservience); and those decades, by contrast, that were troubled and, in some way, dark and tumultuous – times of war, revolts, pestilence, hunger – corresponding to what some years ago was (and continues to be) defined, not without controversy, as "the crisis of the fourteenth century" and to its protracted wake (only three profiles, but of extraordinary women: a princess pilgrim, a writer actually regarded as a witness to her time, and a girl-warrior whose actions are in point of fact not only an enigma, but especially a "*passé qui ne passe pas*," a "past that doesn't pass").

In that this history of famous women is a feminine history, maybe even a history about the many complexities of femininity, it is not at all a "feminist history." We are dealing with an author not in the least interested in what is fashionable, notably with regard to sex or gender. Hers is truly a history on the grand scale: a history always problematic, never erudite or narrative; a history centred on eight women protagonists, but not limited to them; and a history which does not end with them. If, as is oft repeated, and perhaps not mistakenly, behind every great man there is always a great woman, then here it is shown that behind every great woman not only is there always a great man, but often there is more than one. Behind Hildegard, besides secretary Volmar and thanks to him, we glimpse Bernard and Frederick Barbarossa. Raingarde lives not only off the love of her great son, that Peter, Abbot of Cluny, commonly known as "the Venerable," like Bede the Venerable, but she also lives in the intense and passionate memory of her husband Maurice, prematurely taken from her. And it is yet again Peter the Venerable, and not just Peter Abelard, who confers deeper meaning onto Heloise's experiences. Eleanor holds sway not just over Louis VII of France, who becomes almost pitiful when confronted with her charm and energy, but also over the harsh and icy Henry II of England, and over his melancholy and cruel son Richard, who sleeps at her side in the tomb of Fontevrault. Clare is inseparable from Francis and from his teachings, and yet her personality throws a special light on Brother Leo and – especially, since it is something unexpected if not hoped for – on Brother Elias. Bridget of Sweden appears to be deeply marked not only by her not-always-tranquil marriage to Ulf, but by the encounter with her cherished Master Matthias, and by the secretaries who set down in writing her fiery visions, as well as by King Magnus and, finally, by Alfonso de Vadaterra (and it is still difficult to fully determine the influence on her life of the fate of her son Karl – for a brief period lover of Joanna I of Naples – who died prematurely). Christine de Pizan, orphaned at a young age and then widowed, wins the support of Jean Gerson and of Marshal Boucicaut with her celebrated dispute on the subject of the *Roman de la Rose*. As for Joan, who remains a mystery like few other historical characters, there is certainly no man among those who, in some way or other, cross her path – from the weak and uncertain

Charles the Dauphin to the cynical and ambiguous bishop, university rector, and judge Cauchon – who seems to me to reach her stature, except, of course, Phillip, Duke of Burgundy. And yet, I must confess, I would like to know more about the effect that her gaze, or the touch of her hands, had on one of her lieutenants, someone who had been threatened since early childhood by the dark shadow of the horror that would later engulf him. On this subject, I think that Michel Tournier has grasped perhaps something close to a truth, which no one will ever fully uncover. And I am alluding to Gilles de Rais.

The above serves as a description of the first part; the second part can be depicted as perhaps less "strong," but it is more complex, more problematic. Here the safe and trusted guide of the trace left upon history by eminent protagonists is abandoned, and we move on to a different type of record, in which environments, contexts, communities, and maybe even anonymous collective forces govern. We must throw aside an unfortunate and still current prejudice: this is not at all a book tempted by the schizophrenic dichotomy between "big history" and "minor or local history," or any other way we might like to define it. These categories – major and minor history – do not exist: good history exists, written in direct and constant contact with sources, and in the light of the most qualified critical debate, and bad history also exists, history that is second- or third-hand, and which confuses erudition, information, and much-needed intimate understanding with judgmental abuse.

Through her "ordinary women," Maria Teresa Brolis enters into a history no longer dominated by forceful and shrewd personalities, but rather one characterized by the contribution of lively and sensible presences, whose existence is illuminated – but never in a complete or uniform way – by documentary evidence that the author examines with great care, with an attentive critical consciousness, and sometimes with distinctly real and sympathetic affection. The true protagonist of this part of the book is Bergamo itself and its surrounding territory: it is here that Maria Teresa, an eminent connoisseur of archive documents, exercises her powers of bringing old tales back to life. And here we have Giovanna, called Flora, transplanted into nearby Trezzo, and her last will and testament, which resonates indirectly with political passions, and makes restitution for past episodes of usury. Consider the story of the domestic servant Agnesina, a very young orphan, betrothed to the *famulus* (family servant) Paciolo, who is, like her, also impecunious. In order to procure the necessary dowry, Agnesina is aided along with 254 other indigent girls by the town's Confraternity of Mercy (Confraternita della Misericordia); and, beginning with Agnesina, we are afforded a patient and generous statistical-prosopographic study of many other cases of poverty, and small stories of charity granted and received. Take note of the parchment written in 1309 by a notary, under the dictation of Ottebona Uliveni, who was making her will, even if she wasn't sure of being on the verge of death, but who was no longer young or carefree. She was living in forced separation from her husband, in exile for political reasons, and was therefore obligated to rely upon the protection of a legal guarantor, a *mundualdus*, according to Longobard judicial tradition. We have the thirteenth-century story of Grazia d'Arzago, a noble descendant of a family of vassal status, and the abbess of the nunnery of Santa Grata in Bergamo: "a sort of local Hildegard von Bingen," comments the author – a devoted admirer of Hildegard – when describing the activities of this director and reformer of her nunnery, who originally inaugurated it as a "lay" institution of the Confraternity of the Misericordia. Around this woman is organized the complex and even, shall we say, troubled history of an extensive, varied, and lively female religious movement within Bergamo and its rural surroundings, the operations of which are closely interwoven with the political, social, and productive activities of the region. And then there is the glowing and elegant tale of the noblewoman Gigliola dei Suardi, of the great chivalric and Ghibelline family in Bergamo, whose will (drafted in 1327) dazzles us with the splendour of her *guarnazzone* (a type of cloak with sweeping expansive sleeves, covering the entire body of the wearer), perhaps lined with fur, with the blue hue of her dress decorated with silver buttons, and with the multi-coloured coverings of her bed: from this it is not possible to resist the temptation to go off on a fascinating voyage into the world of fashion in that era, obviously based on other trousseaux and other wills, on an excursion that would very much please Maria Giuseppina Muzzarelli (professor of medieval history at the University of Bologna), who, like Maria Teresa, is an aficionado of Hildegard von Bingen and Christine de Pizan; and with an insistence on and a sensitivity to colour which would delight Michel Pastoureau (French scholar and professor of medieval history and the history of Western symbolism). We must also consider the healer Bettina – in the year 1371, in the mountains around the Val Seriana (the Seriana Valley) – a widow who exercises her delicate and, in some respects, risky profession in an age marked by crisis (the Black Death of 1347–51, and recurring wars and famines), and who perhaps – and expectedly – is something more, or at least different, than a country doctor, because she seems to be able to speak with the dead. It is for this reason that she becomes the object of the burdensome attention of the bishop of Bergamo's deputy, not so much because she is suspected of being a witch (witch trials began to take on a specific character in this period and they would crop up from this time up until mid-century), but because it was conjectured that heresy, already encountered in the Bergamo region, was hidden beneath certain false superstitions. Let us also reflect on Margherita de Pillis, recorded in a document from 1399 for having ministered at length and with great dedication to her husband, daughters, and mother-in-law: something that, through her protracted daily exercise of family charity, is testimony to "how daily life can assume a heroic character," as Maria Teresa comments, with an inflection that reveals a profound and even autobiographical sensitivity. And finally we encounter Belfiore, the pilgrim, on the road towards Rome, in the spring of the Jubilee year, 1350, during the full onset of the plague epidemic: again it is a will that tells us of her decision to become a pilgrim and to embark on this trip to Rome, just like other women: for instance the four women Agnese, Giuliana, Caterina, and Romana, from Verona, all widows, who, in 1410, get set to leave for the Holy Land; from this point begins a small but precious (especially, I must confess, for me) investigation into other Venetian, Ligurian, and Tuscan women pilgrims of the fourteenth and fifteenth centuries, as well as earlier.

It has been said that the historian is like the ogre in the fairy-tale: wherever he/she senses the odour of human flesh, he/she knows that there he/she will find a meal. Maria Teresa is an admirable, graciously insatiable ogre that moves with an elegant but implacable nimbleness through her wills, her inventories, her archival documents, and among shiny silver buttons, curious and at times disturbing prescriptions of "popular" medicine, political struggles, and pilgrimages. Here we have a book capable of juxtaposing the rigours of research with the freshness and simplicity of narrative content, as far from the pedantry of a certain type of academicism as it is from didactic oversimplification.

Franco Cardini

ACKNOWLEDGMENTS

I would like to thank McGill-Queen's University Press for
having accepted my book for publication, Sandro Chierici for
his valuable collaboration, and the translator, Joyce Myerson,
because, on reading these pages, she has also read into my soul.
I am deeply honoured and grateful to Professor Giles Constable
(Princeton, Institute for Advanced Study) who wrote the foreword to the English edition of my book.

STORIES OF WOMEN IN THE MIDDLE AGES

INTRODUCTION

For paradox exists everywhere in reality, before existing in thought.
It is everywhere in permanence.
— Henri De Lubac

This book offers up eight stories of famous women and eight biographical sketches of ordinary ones, all of whom lived in that era which we continue to call the Middle Ages.

The first ones made their mark on the larger history of Europe between the twelfth and fifteenth centuries. The others conducted their lives mostly in anonymity in a provincial city of Northern Italy during the fourteenth century.

In some cases, a hundred books world-wide have been written about the first group, all of which have been based on celebrated sources – epistolary correspondences, the chronicles of the time, trials, or at times, the literary works written by the women themselves. The others have just surfaced now or recently, from archival documents: parchments, notarial records, and especially last wills and testaments. Often we are only dealing with fragments, like fragments of fresco painting.

Why then this utterly mismatched juxtaposition?

Because there is a need to know; to investigate the female condition at the centre and on the periphery of the medieval world; to bring together large-scale history with what should never be called local history, in the narrow and restricted sense of the word.

However, these three reasons only partly justify my research. In fact, I do not presume to insert myself with unshakeable certainties into an extremely vast and complex historiographic debate, such as the ongoing decades-long one about medieval women. I believe I have already provided some small but significant scientific contribution to this debate, by publishing in 2001, for the École Française de Rome, the list of almost two thousand women who were registered between 1265 and 1339 in a Lombard confraternity (charitable) association (with an edition born out of the collaboration between Giovanni Brembilla, Micaela Corato, and the teachings of Attilio Bartoli Langeli); and by publishing with Andrea Zonca, in 2012, about fifty wills of Bergamasque women between 1253 and 1399.

But with this book, I address not only the specialists (evidenced also by the brevity of the text). My intention is born of a different aspiration. Franco Cardini identified and outlined it better than I can, in his book on Francis of Assisi (1989), when he said: "Francis does not need biographers ... the biographers need Francis."

And so it is with "my" women: I need them.

They have accompanied me for thirty years – like Hildegard, Heloise, and Raingarde, whom I "met" in the eighties of the last century, during the time of my master's and doctoral theses. Or I encountered them more recently while searching through women's wills in the archives. It is in this way that I found Belfiore, who in 1350 wished to go to Rome, despite the fact that the plague was still a factor, and she would have to traverse half of Italy from north to south. And then came Flora, a usurer, who then changed her life, donating a large part of her riches to the poor, and ordering, as well, that a hot soup made of chickpeas, cooked in an earthenware pot, be distributed to them. And after Flora and Belfiore, there came many others.

Convinced (along with many friends and colleagues) that an historian needs a sense of sympathy towards the subject of his/her study, I openly declare that these women definitely enjoy my sympathy, whether they be saints like Hildegard or Clare, or controversial figures, like the great Heloise, or the little usurer, or even awkward, like Bettina, the visionary healer, about whom we will speak.

I hope that the reader, too, will become captivated, and thus participate in this sympathy.

Additional clarifications could prove useful in introducing this colourful feminine world that the sixteen short tales outline.

If, from a chronological viewpoint – as already hinted at – in the section dealing with the famous women, the period under consideration stretches from the twelfth to the fifteenth centuries (deliberately excluding the Early Middle Ages), and in the second part we concentrate mostly on the fourteenth century, then, from a geographical perspective, the difference between the two sections is more obvious: we proceed from preeminent cities such as Paris, London, Byzantium, and Mainz to a Lombard urban centre, Bergamo, which, while not unimportant in the Late Middle Ages, in terms of economy and culture, is certainly not as renowned and distinguished as the European and Mediterranean localities examined in the first part. The choice depends on two simple factors: on the one hand, the Bergamasque area constitutes the predominant focus of my archival research, and, on the other, this city has afforded profuse documentary surprises in terms of the history of medieval women, in particular with the above-mentioned roster of female confraternity members, which still represents, in terms of numerical consistency and dating, a unique specimen in Europe.

Not only that: in the two sections of text, the sources, and consequently the style, change entirely. It is useful to reiterate this. The research into ordinary women will, in fact, guide the reader towards a type of documentation – the notarial kind – that may seem dry at first, but which reveals identities otherwise elusive. If one cannot find the name of a poor woman in the chronicles of kings, one can read it on a list of beneficiaries in a last will and testament. And it is precisely from women's wills that the narrative, with respect to the ordinary women (Flora, Agnesina, Ottebona, Grazia, Gigliola, Bettina, Margherita, and Belfiore), will mostly emerge, and open out onto analogous cases and themes that their story suggests: from wealth to poverty, from conjugal love to the love of community, from the bedroom to life on the streets.

At this point a slight *excursus* (diversion) into the Bergamasque town and territory in the Middle Ages is necessary to better understand the second half of the text.

Bergamo, nestled on the last rocky spur of the Orobie Prealps, is located in northeastern Lombardy. During the period of the medieval Communes, it was still a small to mid-sized city, extending over a walled area of about thirty hectares, and containing about 15–20,000 inhabitants. The city centre dominates the surrounding countryside, delineated by the borders of the Adda River to the west and the Oglio River to the east; the rivers wend their way north into the valleys of the Prealps, dedicated to sheep-herding, mining, and manufacturing, and descend to the south into the lower Po Valley, which is based on an agricultural economy.

Bergamo, traditionally pro-imperial, ally of Cremona, and rival to Milan and Brescia, became established as a Commune at the beginning of the twelfth century and lasted until 1331, when the Seigniory years began, and it quickly became hegemonized by the Milanese Visconti family. From 1296 through to the end of the fourteenth century, Bergamasque society was shaken by a struggle between political factions, characterized by an almost tribal violence. In particular, the cast-out Guelphs carried out raids in the valleys and the Ghibellines (led by the Suardi family) held their centre of power in the city.

The Church of Bergamo, after the fall of the schismatic bishop Arnolfo in 1098, encountered a revival of Episcopal authority thanks to two exponents of reform, traditionally called "Gregorian": Ambrogio of Mozzo, called "the Patarino," and Gregorio, killed *de gladio* (by the sword) in 1146, both connected to the monastery of Astino. Monasticism had not experienced exceptional expansion compared to other areas of medieval Lombardy: besides an ancient female cenobium in the city (Santa Grata), three Cluniac foundations in the territory, and some small communities of nuns, it was necessary to look forward to the first decade of the twelfth century to see, near the gates of the urban area, in the Valley of Astino, the rise of the Vallombrosan Monastery of San Sepolcro, which would give new stimulus to the religious life of the city. In the second half of the 1100s, the blossoming of numerous hospital communities and the widespread diffusion of the evangelical movement of the Humiliati throughout the diocese would bring further renewal, until, in the thirteenth century, the arrival of the Mendicant Orders and the expansion of the confraternities would provide a decisive impetus to the history of the Church and Bergamasque society.

From a cultural point of view, there was, at the time, an active presence of numerous teachers, writers, and lawmakers in Bergamo. I offer here only two of the most famous examples: in the twelfth century, Mosè del Brolo, who wrote the *Liber Pergaminus*, which belongs to a specific literary tradition – the poetry of praise for a medieval commune; and in the fourteenth century, Alberico da Rosciate, a jurist and friend of Petrarch. Only recently has there been discovered in Bergamo a manuscript representing the oldest evidence of the Sicilian School of poetry: it is the umpteenth proof of the great fortune enjoyed by Northern Italy in the area of the gentle poetry that was transferred from the Provençal poets into the first literary experiences in the vernacular.

My desire to communicate with a larger public motivated me to reduce the documentary and bibliographic references to the essential; these are set down in the final pages under Sources and Bibliography (chapter by chapter), for possible further in-depth study.

And finally the most pleasurable task of all: the acknowledgments.

In gratefully naming all the many people who have been close to me in these years of research and study, and who have contributed to my work, I do not intend to attribute to any one of them the oversights, interpretations, or errors whose responsibility belongs entirely to me. I know that the writing of this book has involved some risks, but my position as an independent scholar allows me a certain amount of relaxed, adventurous, and delightful freedom.

I will begin with the three friends to whom this book is dedicated, with a desired and initial paradox: a text on women dedicated to men!

But Henri De Lubac teaches us: Life is a web of paradoxes.

Franco Cardini believed in this project. He proposed it to the publisher. He wrote the foreword. He reread every chapter, suggesting significant improvements. Since 1987, Franco has inexplicably honoured me with his friendship, and even though we see each other rarely, his respect has given me courage in difficult times. I have no words with which to express my gratitude to him.

Together with him, Attilio Bartoli Langeli reviewed the sections based on notarial documents. In 1998, he became a second teacher and "big brother" to me (I hope he accepts this role). Without his help I could never have brought to fruition the critical edition of some very demanding sources, nor would I have been able to interpret them.

The third friend to whom I dedicate this book is Marco Rossi, someone who broadened my horizons towards the history of medieval art, a particularly beloved field of study for me, through the unshakeable conviction that Beauty has an extraordinary cognitive value. Along with his wife Marisa, Marco has supported me with regards to family relationships, helping me in my attempt to reconcile research and "domestic life."

Further advice on various parts of the book was provided by others who have shared their distinguished knowledge gleaned over a thirty-year period of scholarship.

I would like to most gratefully acknowledge Giuseppina De Sandre Gasparini, whom I consider an expert, for her historiographic refinement and gentle humanity. Her colleague, Maria Clara Rossi, also helped me with various suggestions, granting me the honour of participating on the scientific advisory panel of a journal that I greatly admire: *Quaderni di storia religiosa*. As for other "Venetians," to whom I am also bound by the affinity with the method of the lately lamented Paolo Sambin, I recall with fondness and gratitude Antonio Rigon and Gian Maria Varanini, to whom I add a special group of advisors: Giampaolo Cagnin, Silvia Carraro, Gian Piero Pacini, and Fernanda Sorelli. With respect to the Lombard circle, I will never forget my first teacher, Piero Zerbi, who directed me towards medieval studies, introducing me to that extraordinary figure, Peter the Venerable. The chapters on Raingarde and Heloise bear the effects of that time and constitute a "first love" that one never forgets. Thanks to my training at Milan's Università Cattolica del Sacro Cuore, where I found distinguished guides such as Annamaria Ambrosioni and Maria Pia Alberzoni, I have had occasion to broaden my horizons in terms of non-Italian historiography, through having met two extremely important people in the United States: besides the unforgettable James Powell (Syracuse University), I am referring to Giles Constable (Institute for Advanced Study), who hosted me twice in Princeton, listening to questions, reflections, and requests for help, and who, to this day, by means of a mutual and uninterrupted correspondence, encourages me to especially study ordinary women, about whom – as he maintains and writes – we know little, and whose acquaintance could alter some entrenched judgments on the female condition in the Middle Ages. For this book, as well, Giles has provided me with noteworthy advice, particularly in reference to Abelard, Heloise, and Raingarde.

For questions of economic history and the legal capacities of women, I often consulted Patrizia Mainoni, to whom is due a special thank-you. For medieval theology, I have recently found an authoritative interlocutor in Marco Rainini, who was kind enough to reread the chapter on Hildegard, sharing with me the results of his important research on this subject.

To the rest, whom I will now list in alphabetical order, in the hope of remembering each and every one, I express my sincere acknowledgment of their bibliographical recommendations, shared reflections, and encouragements: Giuliana Albini, Marco Bartoli, Alessandra Bartolomei Romagnoli, Anna Benvenuti, Giovanni Brembilla, Matthias Bürgel, Sandro Chierici, Gianmarco De Angelis, Valeria De Fraja, Carlo Delcorno, Anna Esposito, Maria Grazia Fornaroli, Angiola Locatelli, Franca Longoni, Liliana Maggioni, Francesca Magnoni, Alfonso Marini, Marina Montesano, Angela Orlandi, Lorenzo Paolini, Dario Personeni, Valeria Polonio, Marco Robecchi, and Andrea Zonca.

Finally I wish to thank my children, Anna and Francesco, for having patiently put up with a mother who dedicated so much energy to writing, without, however, wanting to deprive them of my love.

PART ONE

FAMOUS WOMEN

CHAPTER ONE

HILDEGARD

THE GENIUS

She achieved or surpassed the cultural erudition of many men. She spoke with authority to popes and emperors. She preached to the people. She dictated books on theology, physics, alchemy, and cosmology (besides approximately 300 letters in answer to whoever asked her advice). She composed music of surprising beauty. Faced with the genius of Hildegard von Bingen, it is only natural to be astonished and to ask oneself whether a historian could ever unravel the enigma of this woman, who lived in the region of the Rhine River, in the diocese of Mainz, between 1098 and 1179.

We know that during this extraordinary twelfth century, other women were cultured and famous: if, for instance, Heloise (1100–1164), who studied in Paris with her philosopher lover Abelard, especially astounds us with her literary culture, and if Elisabeth of Schönau (1124–1169) lived similar prophetic experiences (to mention two of her celebrated contemporaries), nevertheless Hildegard possessed something special and unique, because she was interested in everything, because she embraced diverse realms of knowledge, and because she united a refined intelligence with an overwhelming passionate nature and an acute emotional force.

In order to shed light on her mystery, I would be tempted to hypothesize a very radical alternative: either the version of her life offered by Hildegard herself is true, namely that God revealed everything to her in a vision, or the reality is that some medieval women were indeed able to attain an extraordinary degree of culture (a premise not yet fully endorsed by all historians).

Despite the fact that interest in the Abbess of Bingen has recently intensified, and that writings about her have multiplied (there is also the 2009 Margarethe von Trotta film), the best introduction to Hildegard is still that of Peter Dronke, who dedicates a chapter to her in his beautiful book on medieval feminine culture: a volume published in 1984 but which should have no fear of the passage of time. This English scholar has identified the essential characteristics of a wide-ranging erudition, gathering what this "Rhenish Sybil" has generated from among the most beautiful flowers of a boundless meadow. We are indebted to him because it is so difficult to venture forth without a guide into Hildegard's entire oeuvre, while worthy specialists have often depicted individual aspects of her knowledge (as our own Marta Cristiani, Michela Pereira, Maria Teresa Fumagalli, and Marco Rainini have done and do quite well).

As a layperson open to religious feeling, Dronke entertains a great admiration for Hildegard, she who "writes in a Latin full of strength and colour, at times subtle and brilliant, reaching the highest standards of the twelfth century": only in very few passages does Dronke wander, in my opinion, from this erudite identification. This happens when he insists on Hildegard's mysticism, placing it in opposition to her scientific curiosity or her love for the earthly, and when he suggests that a sort of "Manichaean dualism" sometimes surfaces in her. It is not, in my opinion, necessary to maintain at all costs that a Christian personality is dualistic, when, identifying with the logic of the Incarnation, one considers creation – that is, the work of a Creator – as lovable.

Let us now briefly look at this great woman's principal stages of life. Born in 1098 in Bermersheim near Alzey (diocese of Mainz), Hildegard belonged to a noble family of middle rank. At eight years of age she entered into an annex to the double monastery (for men and women) of Disibodenberg, where her teacher was Jutta, a young aristocratic woman (daughter of Count Stephen of Spanheim) who had chosen some form of a hermit's life, dedicated to the Holy Scriptures and prayer. We are not entirely sure what sources were available to Jutta, but she passed on to Hildegard a solid preparatory education which she would continue to expand upon in subsequent years.

Whatever the case, this slender little girl, both melancholy and tremendously tenacious, began to learn things that were only circulating in the major centres of culture of the period: for this versatility of knowledge and interests, Dronke even likens her to Avicenna, the famous Persian doctor, physicist, and philosopher of the eleventh century, although he hypothesizes that Hildegard might never have read Avicenna's writings. And in fact, the young Rhenish nun did not only draw from a written culture for her education, but also from listening to other minds (which she then processed with her own great mind), such as the "high-profile scholars that she had to take lessons with, especially – but not exclusively – within the circle of the monasteries associated, in varying degrees, with the Hirsau Reforms" (Rainini): a hypothesis, this latter one, which, after studying Dronke, I believe to be the most convincing ever formulated on the education of Hildegard.

When this young woman decided to stay permanently in the monastery, she quickly showed organizational abilities and an indomitable strength of character. For instance, she tackled the decision, contrary to the opinion of the male community, to found an autonomous convent, that of Rupertsberg, near Bingen, where she became the abbess. At forty years of age, Hildegard obeyed the voice which spoke to her, and she began

to dictate "her" wisdom, to set it down in writing, availing herself of the collaboration of several secretaries. Among these, the
faithful Volmar stands out, as well as the nun Richardis of Stade.
What we have from Hildegard are at least seven volumes, besides
her letters and musical compositions.

The Abbess of Bingen soon became famous not only for her
writings, but for having preached in public outside of the convent, and for having received praise and encouragement from
Pope Eugene III, as well as from that fervent and combative
personage that was Bernard of Clairvaux. The accuser of the
philosopher Abelard would never have endorsed positions that
could even have slightly bordered on heresy, and yet some of
Hildegard's declarations seem truly audacious, such as her references to sexuality, described in reference to the different im-
pulses of the male and female in the moment of their physical
union. Let us read some passages from her book *Causae et Curae*:

> When a woman makes love with a man, feeling a sense of
> warmth in the brain that leads to the joy of the senses, she
> communicates the taste of that delight during the act and
> stimulates the emission of the seed of man. And when the
> seed has fallen into its natural place, that impetuous heat
> descends from the woman's brain and attracts the seed and
> holds it back, and soon the woman's sexual organs con-
> tract and all those parts that are ready to open during the
> menstrual period, now they close, in the same way that a
> strong man can hold something tight in a fist.
>
> ...
>
> When God created Adam, Adam experienced a sense of
> great love in the sleep that God instilled in him. And
> God gave form to that love of the man, and so woman is
> the man's love. And as soon as woman was formed God

gave man the power of creating, that through his love – which is woman – he might procreate children. For when Adam looked on Eve, he was utterly filled with wisdom, for he saw the mother through whom he would beget children. But when Eve looked at Adam, she gazed at him as if she were seeing into heaven, as a Soul which longs for heavenly things stretches upward, for she set her hope in the man, and there will be and there must be the same love, in man and woman, and nothing else. The love of man, compared to that of the woman, is a passionate heat, a fire on blazing mountains, which can hardly be extin-guished, while hers is a small wood fire, easily quenched; but the woman's love compared to that of man is like a sweet warmth proceeding from the sun, which brings forth fruit.

These are expressions of an extraordinary beauty, because they show that a woman can live her virginity as an experience that censures nothing, but is instead an enhancement of the human. Forget sublimation! And yet someone (a moralist or a sceptic) could be scandalized, or not believe that a nun could identify to such a degree with acts she herself had not directly experienced. But Hildegard studied medieval medicine and physics and used their language. She knew the Bible by heart, the Bible whose words are in different moments extremely carnal (eros and agape live together not only in the Song of Songs, but also in some evangelical figures, such as Mary Magdalene), and she observed the world surrounding the cloister; she met the men and women who were connected in some way to the monastic communities (much more than we might think today), and who often came to ask for advice, all the while telling their personal stories. In the twelfth century, the rules of seclusion weren't actually as rigid as they would become in the Late Middle Ages, and we mustn't imagine the female monasteries as "sealed enclosures." Not only that: in certain liturgical celebrations, Hildegard wanted her nuns to dress in white, wearing crowns on their heads, just like noble young girls out in the world, because the brides of Christ had to be beautiful and so would their song be beautiful, accompanied by the same kinds of musical instruments used in celebrations at court. Sometimes the convent held theatrical sacred representations, according to theatrical forms which had interested the cloistered communities for centuries, in various ways: proof of this exists all the way from Hrotsvitha's literary and erudite forms through to those humble and popular ones of the "Little Flower" Thérèse, who would impersonate Joan of Arc within the Carmelite community in Lisieux.

Hildegard's artistic research also demonstrates how open the religious experience was in the twelfth century, through her gentle and "courtly" notations, and through the effective proof of the mutual influence of diverse mentalities.

These choices were obviously not shared by everyone. Besides the usual misogynistic moralists, Tengwind, the mother superior of another female convent along the Rhine (Andernach), came forward, shocked as she was by these theatrical representations, which she considered worldly, and accused Hildegard of imitating the style of the nobility, invoking the pauperistic model as the obligatory lifestyle for nuns: hers is a protest letter to Hildegard demanding explanations. These accusations were in part dictated by jealousy as well, considering the growing success of the Bingen community, and, in fact, by a particular problem: Hildegard's choice to accept only girls of noble birth in her convent – a controversial choice, but commendable in its results, because art in Bingen played the leading role in monastic life.

In order to understand Hildegard, it is perhaps necessary to listen to the melodies and words she composed in certain texts

(*O magne Pater* or *Ave generosa*): these songs are evidence of how Beauty was central to her life, and how it may have embodied an artistic and religious need to communicate in so many different ways.

A similar sensitivity is also traceable in the harmony that Hildegard sought between macrocosm and microcosm, a popular tendency in the "scientific" culture of the period. Even some of her writings on herbal medicine and her culinary recipes reflect this passion to find the Beautiful and the Good in simple little things, from spelt to chervil, and in other plants or herbs.

The Abbess of Bingen did not spend her whole life in the cloister. Several great figures of the period continued to consult her, putting her to the test. In these instances, too, the tenacity of a woman who knew how to respond with agility and vitality surprises us, although from the standpoint of her health she was weak; besides suffering from persistent migraine, she was, in fact, often bedridden, even seriously ill.

The force with which Hildegard reproached Emperor Frederick I for having nominated an anti-pope is astounding. Her words are vehement: "You have behaved like a fool [*stultus*]." Only the imperial authority could thwart the reaction of the faithful, who wanted to burn down the monastery of Bingen to avenge the offence.

Towards the end of her long life, Hildegard, a second Antigone, faced another terrible battle; she refused to give up to others the corpse of a noble knight, who, sick and penitent, had been nursed, and then buried in the convent cemetery. Before dying, the nobleman became reconciled with the Church, but some prelates from nearby Mainz, in the absence of the archbishop who was in Rome, claimed that Hildegard had housed an excommunicated individual. This time the ordeal proved extremely hard, because the disobedient abbess was subjected to a ban, and silence was imposed on the community. Hildegard's inflammatory letter, sent to the priests of Mainz, represents the extraordinary evidence not only of her courageous awareness of being in the right, but also of her love for song and music, which she considered honoured practices for entering into relationship with God.

> Thus you and all other prelates must use the greatest care
> before silencing with a decree any assembly of people
> raising their voices to God ... you must always take care
> not to be deceived in your judgements by Satan, who
> diverted mankind away from celestial harmony and the
> joys of paradise.

From this perspective, Hildegard's thought is decidedly not anomalous, because even in the Cluniac tradition, liturgical music played a central role: the abbot of Cluny, Peter the Venerable, in a letter sent to two of his nieces, recognized that women's song had an extraordinary and charismatic efficacy, even comparable to preaching, which was reserved for men.

Just six months before her death, Hildegard was able to once again hear music within the walls of her convent, because the archbishop of Mainz, writing from Rome, sided with her and dismissed the ban. Thus Hildegard's written words, addressed to Mary in the hymn *Ave generosa*, once more sounded forth:

> How deep is that delight that God received in you,
> when 'round you he enwrapped his warm embrace,
> so that his Son was suckled at your breast.
>
> Your womb rejoiced
> as from you sounded forth the whole celestial symphony.
> For as a virgin you have borne the Son of God –
> in God your chastity shone bright.

Hildegard uses terms that remind us of those that Dante would direct to the "Virgin Mother" in the last canto of the *Paradise*: "Within your womb rekindled was the love / that gave the warmth that did allow this flower / to come to bloom within this timeless peace." It is a long-distance dialogue between two great geniuses, a woman and a man, who have left their mark on the history of Western culture.

Long considered "blessed," and the object of veneration of a local cult, Hildegard von Bingen was proclaimed a saint by Benedict XVI on 10 May 2012, and immediately afterwards (7 October) was counted among the Doctors of the universal Church.

CHAPTER TWO

RAINGARDE

THE MOTHER

The castle of Montboissier where Raingarde lived is now a basalt quarry, in the vicinity of a village (Brousse) located on the green uplands of the central Auvergne region, between the towns of Ambert and Issoire. A similar fate was inflicted upon the monastery of Cluny, where the son of Raingarde, Peter the Venerable, was the abbot for thirty-four years (1122–56), becoming one of the most celebrated intellectuals of his era: at the end of the eighteenth century, when the church (as large as St Peter's in Rome) was destroyed, the area became a stone quarry, and even today whoever visits this beautiful place in Bourgogne will find it difficult to retrieve among the abbey ruins a memory of this great man, who so resembled his mother.

Raingarde's story has been handed down to us in a long letter written by Peter as a form of consolation for himself and his brothers, after her death in 1134; the letter is known to medieval studies largely because of Giles Constable, who did the critical edition, and Peter von Moos, who included it in a comprehensive and complex study dedicated to the medieval consolatory literary genre. On the basis of their excellent analysis, it is possible (and rightly so!) to consider the central section of the text (the so-called *Narratio*) as a biographical source. It tells the tale of a remarkable woman, though one little known outside a specialized niche (only one monographic essay on Raingarde appeared in Italy in 1963, thanks to Paolo Lamma). It is appropriate to insist on the historical rather than just the literary character of this source for two reasons: on the one hand, even though it may also have a hagiographic and commemorative connotation, the text incorporates genuine biographical passages (in part confirmed by other documents); on the other, it is configured as an interesting testimony to filial love towards a mother, offering us a vivid and penetrating image, filled with intimate affection, of her and her life. The Middle Ages has left us moving testimonies of mothers writing to their long-lost sons, from Dhuoda (ninth century) to Alessandra Macinghi Strozzi (1407–1471). Here, instead, it is a son who writes of the mother, and through his words, we can understand how intense and nuanced was the perception of this same maternal figure in the thinking of that time.

Raingarde was married to Maurice II of Montboissier, a member of the upper-middle-class aristocracy of Auvergne, and bore him eight children. The two spouses had strong ties to the Church of the Auvergne, demonstrated by their financial support of the Cluniac priory of Sauxillanges, where young Peter began his religious training. This tendency was part of a well-established family tradition, even documented by an event in the life of one of Peter the Venerable's ancestors, Maurice, who, having gone to Rome with his wife, had contributed a substantial amount to the foundation of the church of San Michele alla Chiusa on his return.

The Auvergne is a terrain of wide open spaces, of green mountains, and of rocky spurs upon which sit the religious buildings that tower above the pilgrimage routes. Even Peter's father undertook a trip, not, however, towards Rome or Santiago de Compostela, but to Jerusalem, having decided to participate in the First Crusade. During his absence, Raingarde exercised the responsibility of *domina loci*, of castellan, knowing full well how to govern and manage the lands entrusted to her. In many ways her story is similar to those of many other wives of crusaders who, finding themselves in similar situations, learned how to administer the family properties.

Even after her husband's return, Raingarde continued to be active by his side, as evidenced in some documents of the Sauxillanges cartulary. Among the prerogatives that she exercised there was also the one her son described with polite irony as "an indiscreet welcoming of guests," applied towards various categories of people, including wandering monks. This inclination of his mother (according to Peter) was not always guided by a criterion of moderation, whether in terms of the frequency of her hospitality, or by the welcoming of some rather unusual individuals. For instance, a rather famous person in the female religious world of the time, as well as among the secular grandes dames, was received in Montboissier: Robert d'Arbrissel, founder of Fontevrault, namely that double monastery in which the women governed and guided the male community. "*Famosus ille*" ("that famous one"), Peter wrote in relation to Robert's visit, not hiding his puzzlement over new forms of religious life that often stood in contrast to, or in competition with, the established Cluniac tradition.

Raingarde had been subjected to the allure of this itinerant preacher, and did not hide from her husband her desire to become a nun, with his approval, actually together with him, albeit in different communities, according to the practice of the *conversio coniugatorum* (the conversion of the spouses). Peter's narrative presents his father as a benevolent and patient man with respect to the often impulsive fervour of his wife, who, however, had to alter her plans because of the serious illness that afflicted the lord of Montboissier. It was 1117 and the son, Peter, was present in the ancestral home during a scene that would become indelibly imprinted on his memory.

Statuesque, self-denying, unconditionally striving to achieve the salvation of her husband, Raingarde sits beside the bed of her dying spouse. Behind her motionless face, her soul, however, is in agitation, and in order to allow Maurice to prepare himself for life's most decisive meeting without worries, she prepares his will in his presence. She settles the disputes, appoints the heirs, divides the castles, and puts everything in order down to the smallest detail. It is obvious that the image of the virago, the *foemina virilis*, of the woman who demonstrates a composure and a courage superior to that of men, is present here according to the forms and features of a model that boasts an ancient philosophical and literary tradition; it is also true that Peter's story reveals some peculiar and original characteristics, indicative of a restless female personality who undoubtedly influenced him a great deal.

In this regard, one can find some particularly effective expressions in the text referring to the protagonist's character: the impulsiveness and the fervent emotional nature of the mother are suggested more than once by phrases such as *"impulsa violento aestu animi"* ("driven by the passionate fervour of her spirit"), *"facibus ardebat"* ("she was inflamed"), and *"fervens spiritu animus requiescere nesciebat"* ("her spirit, so full of ardour, could not find peace"). Even after Maurice's death, Raingarde's attitude reveals a restlessness that is provoked by love (*"amoris stimulis agitate"*), so much so that she increases the number of pilgrimages, prayers, donations to the poor, and offers to intercede, without any rest whatsoever.

Peter thus offers us a portrait that is not at all stereotyped nor linear. Indeed, from his story, what emerges are the striking if not passionate aspects of a spirited woman. This is further expressed in a scene that represents Raingarde beside the grave of her husband, who was buried in Sauxillanges. In fact, after having made the decision to reject any future marriage proposals, and to leave Montboissier to enter into a convent (no longer however in Fontevrault but in the Cluniac Marcigny priory in Bourgogne), during the night before her definitive departure from her domain, the castellan is accompanied by a trusted monk to Sauxillanges, where she spends the night embracing her husband's tombstone, recalling aloud the stages of her married life, and sometimes actually speaking in Maurice's voice. This proves just how much she identified with the man whom she had deeply loved and whom she was leaving for a second time.

"Loquebatur velut ore defuncti, et quasi commutatis personis in coniuge vir paenitebat." ("She was speaking as if in the voice of her husband and, having switched from one to the other, the man confessed through the woman.") This scene did not escape the attention of some scholars who, besides pointing out its evocative power, interpreted the episode in various ways, highlighting either the religious aspects (the will to do penance) or the emotional ones (the sorrow over the loss of conjugal love).

On leaving the Auvergne, Raingarde travelled towards Bourgogne together with her entourage, who accompanied her first to Cluny, and then to Marcigny, where, having said her farewells to relatives, friends, and servants, the Lady of Montboissier entered into a community that then had about one hundred nuns, including the famous Countess Adela of Blois, the daughter of William the Conqueror.

At that time the finances of the priory were not in a great state, and Raingarde was again called upon to serve God more with the industriousness of Martha than with the contemplative acceptance of Mary (two evangelical models recognizable to the mentality of the era). She was then nominated as the cellarer, namely the administrator of the convent, and to undertake this responsibility, she often had to leave the cloister. Even if Peter portrays his mother grappling with the convent's cuisine, intent on satisfying the needs of all her sisters, preparing a varied and careful menu, it is plausible that the guardianship of the monastic assets

Famous Women

in particular would have been the most appropriate task for the ex-castellan of Montboissier. She also lavished advice, based on her management skills and insights, onto her son, who came to see her during the brief pauses amid the intensive work imposed upon him: maintaining and reforming a vast network of monasteries extending from Northern Italy to the Iberian peninsula; confronting the rising success of Cistercian monasticism, often combative towards Cluny; and negotiating with the pope, kings, and other important individuals of his time. Peter's visits to Marcigny offer up glimpses into an uninterrupted dialogue between mother and son, and into the mutual transmission of comfort, affection, and influence.

While Peter was returning from the Council of Pisa, where the schism upsetting the Church was discussed, he received notification of Raingarde's death.

The last part of her life has been gathered from the evidence of the sisters who attended the abbot in Marcigny for the services. It is a scene of particular emotional strength, very powerful in the *descriptio mortis*, obviously based on well-developed literary models, but nevertheless emotionally compelling on an exquisitely human level. On the bed, in which she lay dying, Raingarde had asked to have a cross to kiss, and from which she did not wish to disengage her lips, as if she had substituted the symbolic representation for Him who was the true object of her love: "*Ita non imaginem sed ipsum in cruce illa se videre reputans, ab amplexu eius divelli non poterat*" ("So, believing that she was seeing not the image but the actual Person on the cross, she would not let herself be torn from the embrace").

This gesture calls to mind the embrace at Maurice's grave during the night that preceded Raingarde's departure from the castle of Montboissier: both gestures demonstrate the consummate capacity to convey deep emotion, and to absorb it with empathy, respectively revealing so much of the nature of the one who experienced it, and the one who chronicled it.

CHAPTER THREE

ҺELOISE

THE LOVE-STRUCK

*Under the pretext of study we spent our hours in the happiness of love,
and learning held out to us the secret opportunities that our passion
craved. Our speech was more of love than of the books which lay open
before us; our kisses far outnumbered our reasoned words. Our hands
sought less the book than each other's bosoms — love drew our eyes
together far more than the lesson drew them to the pages of our text.*

Thus writes the lover/professor, one of the most famous philosophers of the Middle Ages: Peter Abelard.

"I, who have experienced so many pleasures in loving you, feel, in spite of myself, that I cannot repent them." So Heloise, the love-struck pupil, recalls after many years. She became, out of obedience, first a wife and then a nun after her forced and violent separation from Peter, the victim of a brutal revenge.

The facts are well-known. Let us summarize them: Paris, 1117, Peter Abelard is giving lessons to a girl of rare beauty and culture, in exchange for free rent in the house of her uncle Fulbert, a canon of Nôtre-Dame, and Heloise's guardian. The two fall in love. For a while their relationship remains secret, until she becomes pregnant, and gives birth to their son Astrolabe (1118), and she reluctantly acquiesces to marrying Abelard, because she doesn't want to harm his career. The wedding is not made public because Abelard has taken minor orders and is a cleric, as was the custom then, especially for teachers of theology; for him, celibacy is not stipulated by law, but highly recommended by tradition. The secrecy of the marriage, however, does not rectify the situation in a satisfying way for the uncle, who complains about it to Heloise; so Abelard makes her dress up as a nun and takes her to the convent of Argenteuil (near Paris), where she had been educated as a young girl. Heloise's relatives believe that the *magister* might want to get rid of the pupil, and so order the atrocious vengeance of the castration of Abelard. The philosopher enters monastic life and compels Heloise to do the same. The two live separately for years, until in 1129 she becomes the abbess of the convent of the Paraclete, founded by Abelard, who ends his days in Cluny (1142) after the censure of his philosophical works.

This is one of the most legendary love stories of European literature, handed down from the testimony of the protagonists, Heloise and Abelard, through the letters they exchanged around 1135. "The problem of a love and a correspondence" is the best form of expression to define the historiographic debate that has involved so many medieval scholars, fascinated by the two figures. During the second half of the past century, someone cast doubt on the authenticity of the correspondence (causing concern in the famous Cluny conference of 1972), and then had a change in idea, and, with intellectual honesty, retracted their suggestive but extremely complicated theory, according to which the letters of Abelard and Heloise were the work of two or more forgers of the twelfth century. With the credibility of the source verified, we can thus draw on it to experience a real story, while taking into account that the literary aspect is always very present in medieval letters, together with the purely biographical data.

The lengthy historiographic controversy nevertheless reveals a deeper issue that cannot be evaded. Could such sensuous and intense language have existed at the time? Could such a love be "chronologically misplaced"? Could a woman of the thirteenth century say – as did Heloise – "If the name of wife appears more sacred and more valid, sweeter to me is ever the word friend, or, if thou be not ashamed, concubine" and ask with apprehension, after a long silence between the two of them, "Was it not the sole thought of pleasure which engaged you to me?"

Heloise's bold words are contemporaneous to those words, fiery and poetic as well, of Hildegard (who lived at the same time), in her writings on the physiology of eros between spouses. The literary education of the two lovers included, from lesson to lesson, Ovid with his *Ars amatoria*, Cicero with his *De amicitia*, or the texts in the courtly repertory that Abelard himself composed and sang successfully in Paris. Some years later, in the same city, Richard of Saint Victor would write the *Tractatus de quatuor gradibus violentae caritatis*, with glowing words about the good of conjugal love, words which reveal a great ability to identify with the various aspects of human affectivity, without indulging in spiritualizing and moralizing. On the themes of amorousness, it was not only biblical imagery that inspired the language of the time, but also that of hagiographic sources that represented the lives of the saints in often quite crude and carnal terms.

In this rich context, therefore, it is not surprising that the *Historia Calamitatum* (the autobiography of Abelard) and the letters between the two lovers circulated without censorship of all those extremely explicit erotic references.

Another aspect of the story, seemingly banal or insignificant, has instead always intrigued me: how could a young laywoman in Paris, raised for a few years in a nunnery, and then in the home of her canon uncle, gain access to private lessons by the most famous university professor at the time? Abelard explains it as if he were the sole architect of the encounter: so taken was he with the girl, who lived near his school, that he convinced her uncle Fulbert to rent him a room in exchange for lessons. But when he met Heloise, "she stood out above all by reason of her abundant knowledge of letters," and it was Fulbert who encouraged her first studies, bringing her to that level of excellence.

The shadow of that dreadful vengeance against the philosopher obviously weighs on Heloise's uncle. For this reason we often forget that at the beginning of the story, before the explosion of scandal in his home, he, too, seems quite impressive: he financed the education of the girl because he loved her. In fact, Abelard recounts the story in this way:

> Now there dwelt in that same city of Paris a certain young girl named Heloise, the niece of a canon who was called Fulbert. Her uncle's love for her was equalled only by his desire that she should have the best education which he could possibly procure for her ... Now he was a man keen in avarice and likewise he was most desirous for his niece that her study of letters should ever go forward.

Why did Fulbert express his love for his niece by making her study? Was Heloise an exceptional creature whom he wished to display like a circus performer before public admiration out of vanity, seeing as – according to Abelard – female literary culture was such a rare quality? But was it actually so rare? By now we know that other women of the period were able to reach an elevated degree of culture and that that quality was appreciated by great personages. Let us look at two extremely decisive figures in the history of this era, ones who assumed different positions with respect to the same Abelard, the first accusing him over his philosophical writing, the second welcoming him with reverent fatherliness to the monastery of Cluny. I am referring to Bernard of Clairvaux and Peter the Venerable. Both have written important words in praise of women, and the Cluniac abbot sent to Heloise a fervent and delicate letter (as he so well knew how to do) with that famous ending so full of hope:

> Now, venerable and dearest sister in the Lord, this man
> to whom you were bound first by the ties of the flesh and
> later by the much stronger and better bond of divine love,
> with whom and under whom you have long served the
> Lord – this man, I say, in your place and as another you,
> Christ cherishes in his own embrace. He holds him to be
> restored to you by his grace at the coming of the Lord,
> when he descends from heaven with the singing of arch-
> angels and the sound of the trumpet.

"This man ... Christ cherished in his own embrace. He holds him to be restored to you" is truly an expression possessing a strong emotional connotation that one should not underestimate. Moreover, I believe that Peter the Venerable may just have found the most beautiful words with which to console Heloise, in comparison to the coldness that certain passages from Abelard's letters betray, provoking what Peter von Moos has defined as the "the silence of Heloise" – the forced renunciation of speaking of their love in order to devote themselves to their common endeavour: the convent of the Paraclete. It is a coldness which, from the theological viewpoint, seems supported by references to a vein of misogyny, recognizable in Abelard's frequent quotes from St Jerome, or from some Old Testament books, such as Ecclesiastes. The choice of sources or biblical models, in terms of intellectual inclinations, is decisive for the understanding of mentality; think of how important the Song of Songs is in the formation of Western mentality around the concept of eros. Twelfth-century monastic theology included highly positive voices in relation to the theme of conjugal love and sexuality, as Jean Leclercq has demonstrated in his very fine essay written in 1982, one which has not enjoyed, in my opinion, the good fortune it deserves.

Unlike Peter the Venerable, Abelard, the greatest expert on words and dialectics of his time, perhaps did not find the right words to console his beloved, and he had to resort to his authority to compel her to silence on the past.

And she obeys. She writes, in fact: "So that you cannot accuse me of disobedience in anything, I have imposed the reining in of your command even on the words of my immeasurable pain."

From here on in, it remains only to comment on the rule of the Oratory of the Paraclete, but something is lost in the enforced sublimation; the love between a man and a woman fades, becomes reduced, in its positive sense, both human and specific. Heloise knows it, and precisely in the letter in which she seems to obey him, accepting the order to be silent on the past, she hides her rebellion by encrypting the words in her salutation: "Suo specialiter, sua singulariter." As if to say: you wish to be mine as a "species" of monk, but I am yours as a single individual, as a woman, with all the history that we have lived together.

CHAPTER FOUR

ELEANOR

THE QUEEN

With Eleanor we can ride through the most beautiful landscapes of the mid-twelfth century, from the golden or colourful fields of her native Aquitaine, land of the troubadours, to the mists and green spaces around Paris and London, the cities of her royal husbands, up to the clear blue of eastern skies surrounding the splendour of Byzantium, or to the fiery yellow of the desert, overwhelming the crusaders in retreat. In Eleanor's entourage we hear the love songs of Bernard de Ventadour, the flutes, the vielle, and the psaltery, the poetry that celebrates woman as the mistress of the heart, but also breaks through the noise of the weapons of war that stabilize or destabilize power.

Wife of two kings, mother of ten princes and princesses, patroness of artists, regent for her son, indomitable traveller: not only few women, but maybe even few men, have had a life as adventurous as hers.

Let us trace the main milestones, allowing the facts to speak for themselves, so intense are they in their drama and splendour.

Niece of the first troubadour, Duke William IX of Aquitaine, Eleanor is born around 1122 in Bordeaux. Her father William X gives her hand in marriage to Louis, the Capetian heir, whom she marries in 1137, bringing him a dowry of a vast territory in southwest France. Soon after the marriage, he is crowned king, with the name Louis VII. The proud and beautiful girl thus finds herself queen at around fifteen years of age, while her husband is only seventeen. In the first years of their reign, impulsivity or stubbornness orient the young couple to a rash and aggressive policy, directed to imposing royal power on the feudal system, until the shameful massacre of the inhabitants of Vitry, burned alive by the king's soldiers inside their church. Louis VII, upset and utterly changed, dresses as a penitent, asking for forgiveness in public, and Eleanor, too, suffers, but also for a more intimate pain: in seven years of marriage, she has not yet had children. For this reason, in 1144, the queen obtains a personal audience with St Bernard de Clairvaux, the most famous and highly regarded man of the Church in that moment. The queen requests his intercession with God. The abbot accepts, seeking, however, the immediate cessation of violence in the kingdom. A year later, her first child, Mary, is born.

But new fronts open up: Edessa has fallen and the same Bernard, upon the request of Eugene III, recommends from his pulpit an expedition to the Holy Land. Eleanor wishes to accompany her husband, after having collected offers from the whole of the dominion to finance the armed expedition. On the road to Palestine in 1147, the French sovereigns are received in Byzantium with all due honour, but the subsequent military campaign turns out to be a total fiasco, and serious conflicts erupt even within the royal couple. Louis VII in fact proceeds alone to Jerusalem, while Eleanor does not want to leave Antioch. On the return to Paris, despite the birth of their second child, Alice, in 1150, the relationship between the two spouses seems irremediably damaged.

In 1152, upon request of the queen, the marriage is annulled on the basis of presumed consanguinity, and Eleanor returns to her Poitiers not without dangers, given that she is escaping from a double attempt at abduction on the part of the Count of

Champagne, interested in taking over her lands. It is the same duchess who, quickly but secretly, begins negotiations for a new marriage that would secure her safety from other unwelcome suitors. In the face of the amazement of many, a wedding is celebrated in May of 1152 between Eleanor and Henry Plantagenet, Count of Anjou and Duke of Normandy, who two years later would become king of England, as well as holding on to a good part of French soil. The spouses then move to London for the coronation, and the queen, now a thirty-year-old, still makes a splendid figure next to her impetuous husband, who is younger than his wife by ten years.

Between 1153 and 1166, Eleanor gives Henry eight children (three girls and five boys), but she does not relinquish her political commitments because of these frequent pregnancies, sharing as she does in the government of the new realm, and even moving many times across the Channel. In the decade of splendour and harmony with Henry, the queen creates a court worthy of its name, from the literary standpoint as well, hosting poets and artists. However, around 1166 (the year of the birth of her last son, the future John Lackland and king of England), signs of unrest begin to cast a shadow. The Plantagenet, in fact, betrays her with the beautiful Rosamund, and in Aquitaine, where the indignant Eleanor has moved, news reaches her of an assassination in Canterbury Cathedral: Archbishop Thomas Beckett has died at the hands of assassins sent by the king. The year is 1170.

The concern is deeply felt all over Europe, and the cult of Thomas the martyr is quickly established despite a monarch who, from this moment on, will have to fight to keep his power, even against his own sons, who rebel against him with their mother's support. It is, in fact, Henry the Young King who leads the revolt, until his premature demise in 1183, at just twenty-eight years of age. The rebellion continues, from Poitiers once again, with Richard, the future Lionheart, at its head; but his father Henry knows how to defend himself well, and is even able to capture Eleanor, who, after twenty years from her first trip to London as bride and queen, crosses the Channel to begin a long, sad period of imprisonment. In vain, her children beg for her freedom, which would be granted only in July 1189, when King Henry II dies, after learning that even his favourite child, John, is united with his enemies.

But life offers no respite to Eleanor. Now it is necessary to protect "her" Richard from the ambitions of his younger brother, and from the continuous conflicts with the new French king. Just after her liberation from prison, the queen mother leaves for Sicily, to the Norman court, where her daughter Joanna lives, and where she is preparing the wedding between Richard and Berengaria, whom he met and praised in poetry at the court of King Sancho of Navarre. After the wedding is celebrated in Cyprus, en route for the Holy Land, Richard undertakes his armed expedition, and shows his true temperament, more combative than poetic; in the siege of St John of Acre, he overshadows the fame of other important leaders (such as Philip Augustus, king of France), without, however, boosting the overall fortunes of the war. After the substantial failure of the expedition, and during the return trip, Richard is made prisoner by the Duke of Austria, inspired by the French king. And it is always Eleanor who moves to collect the enormous sum of money to pay the ransom, to protect Plantagenet rule, to punish the abductors (she would write three letters to the pope to obtain the excommunication of the duke and the ban against Philip of France), and to personally engage in the negotiations that would bring her son to freedom in February of 1194.

The "Queen of Two Crowns" can now withdraw to her beloved Fontevrault, the abbey north of Poitiers, which she had always protected, and to which she had always contributed. Both a male and female monastery, in which the women were always in control over the men, this cenobium has hosted illustrious and cultured abbesses, along with lepers, who were cured in a separate building: Robert of Arbrissel had founded it, dedicating it to Mary Magdalene, and Eleanor – hardly surprising – favours this place over all other monasteries.

News reaches her at Fontevrault – perhaps the saddest of her long life – that Richard is dying from a wound (almost trivial compared to others he has endured) and wishes to see his mother. With only a few years of actual rule behind him, in his prime, and just forty years old, Richard dies in the arms of Eleanor, who reaches him in time, and then accompanies his coffin to the abbey of Fontevrault early in April of 1199.

In two years' time, Marie of Champagne and Joanna meet their deaths before their mother, while the poor government of the last son, John, drags the Plantagenet reign towards crisis and disgrace.

And yet Eleanor once again amazes with her resurgent strength. Though by now an eighty-year-old, she still rides, beyond the Pyrenees, towards her last remaining daughter: Eleanor of Castile, wife of Alphonse VIII. In the Castilian court, the grandmother is met by eleven grandchildren. She chooses and proposes Blanche, a child of eleven, as the wife to the heir of the king of France. This girl would become the future Queen Blanche, mother of the sainted Louis IX.

Returning for good to Fontevrault, would Eleanor again hear the music of her troubadours in the hymns that resonated from the choir? Do not the songs, *Mere au Sauveur* or *Ma viële*, praise God and the Virgin with the same melodies of courtly love poetry? Perhaps we of the modern age have forgotten this, but so it was in that land of poets and warriors: music certainly accompanied the queen on her last ride towards a new horizon that loomed the day of her *Dies Natalis* (day of her death and birth into heaven), in the spring of 1204.

CHAPTER FIVE

CLARE

THE FOUNDER

"*Però che, essendo lei bella de la faccia, se trattava de darle marito*" ("Seeing as she was endowed with a beautiful face, there was discussion about finding her a husband"): so states Messer Ranieri de Bernardo de Assisi, who frequented the family of the nobleman Favarone di Offreduccio from the time his daughter Clare was a child. With this descriptive passage, rare within the sources, Ranieri says (finally!) that the girl was not only "saintly" but also "beautiful"; in particular (he remarks) she had a beautiful face. Out of all the evidence gleaned at her Process of Canonization in 1253 (an exceptional text – not least because it was vernacularized – discovered in 1920), I like to begin with the genteel words of this masculine and courtly compliment, in a story where the love between a man and a woman, a human love, is blended with the love for God.

The young Clare was therefore beautiful, but she did not want to marry, managing to fend off betrothal up to the age of eighteen (not an easy task at that time); she was driven by a steadfast religious aspiration, seconded and nourished by her mother Ortolana, the courageous pilgrim to the Holy Land, and by at least two of her sisters, Catherine and Beatrice. An intense Christian sentiment permeated the Favarone household. Lepers and the poverty-stricken were already part of the life of this girl, who found ways to give or bring food to them, as she observed and judged the world outside her family circle. What could not have escaped her attention was the well-broadcasted story of the son of a merchant, about twelve years older than her, the one who had been "the king of the youth" of Assisi, and who now wished to be instead the "herald of the great King." For quite a while, in his city and its surroundings, Francis, son of Pietro Bernardone, had, in fact, chosen to follow in the footsteps of Christ, living a type of life which, although at first incomprehensible to many, seemed to be attracting anew, but in a different way, various youths of Assisi, including Rufino, Clare's cousin.

The story's development is also treated in the record of the 1253 proceedings: "Wherein she testifies that more than once she went with her to speak with St. Francis, and that she went secretly so as not to be seen by her family" (*Process, Testimony* 17). The person speaking is a laywoman, Bona de Guelfuccio de Assisi, a childhood friend and companion in those meetings during which Francis proposed to Clare "that she convert to Jesus Christ" and to brother Filippo Longo, also present, that "he do the same." Before deciding to leave her family, Clare was therefore already in contact with that original community of Minors, at this point a fraternity of penitents recognized by the Church: in 1209 their lifestyle had been verbally approved of in Rome by Pope Innocent III. But for Bona de Guelfuccio, these men were simply "those who worked at Santa Maria de la Porziuncola," to whom she had, among other things, brought offerings, at Clare's behest, so that they might buy some meat. How beautiful was this gesture of feminine solicitude, one which would be reciprocated in the future, when Francis would invite the Abbess of St Damian to eat a little more, trying to restrict her voluntary fasting. But

Bona would not be present on the night of 1211 (or 1212) when "Clare converted" (in other words when she abandoned her lay status), because the friend would be on pilgrimage to Rome for Lent. It was, in fact, on Palm Sunday, at night, that Clare fled her home, having some difficulty in opening the secondary, less-used door (so say the hagiographers), and ran downhill towards the plain of Assisi where her "brothers" were awaiting her with lit torches. And even with the certainty of historical fact, one should not miss the gender-reversed biblical echo (Matthew 25: 1–13) that shines on the scene: this time it is men who await with their torches the "wise virgin" who has chosen her Bridegroom.

Thus it came true just as Francis had predicted six years earlier, singing in French from the top of a dilapidated roof above a small church in need of repair: "Come and help me in the work of the Church of St. Damian, which shall be a convent of Ladies, by whose good report and life, our celestial Father will be glorified in the universal Church!"

This step – reported in the *Legend of St. Francis by the Three Companions* and in the *Testament of Clare of Assisi* – is the first hint of that "diligent care and special solicitude" that Francis promised, and later executed, in writing, in the *Formula Vitae* (the Little Rule) of the "Poor Ladies" of St Damian (however, the translation "diligent" does not really provide the semantic significance of "love with preference," inherent in the Latin verb *diligo* from which the term derives).

After cutting her hair and putting on the penitential habit, Clare had not yet formulated a definitive and clear way forward. For a short time she remained in the prominent Assisian convent of San Paolo delle Abbadesse, where she was received as a lay-servant and not as a professed nun, from the moment that she sold her dowry to give it to the poor. Afterwards she moved to Sant'Angelo in Panzo, a true community of penitents, where she was joined by her sister Catherine (later called Agnes), whose flight unleashed the wrath of their uncle Monaldo, head of the noble family clan. But he was unable to dissuade either of the two girls from their chosen destiny.

Once Clare had established herself permanently at St Damian, other friends arrived, such as Pacifica, Balvina, and Benvenuta. Clare became their "Mother" for a long period of time: forty-two years, twenty-nine of which she lived in poor health!

After her undeniably adventurous life-changing nocturnal flight, the still-young woman lived days and nights of simple routine, expressed in prayer, in the care of her sisters (eventually numbering about fifty), in the seeking of Christ through the example of Francis, for whom she was the "little plant," as she loved to define herself, and in the obvious self-perception of belonging to the same fraternity as the men.

Incredibly onerous challenges intruded upon this apparent "normality" and they accompanied Clare until her death in 1253, twenty-seven years after that of Francis (1226). I will consider some moments and aspects of these challenges, ones that are particularly indicative of tenacity and faith, as experienced by a woman, who reminds us, although in very different contexts, of the combative tendency already encountered in Hildegard. Clare of Assisi is a *mulier fortis*, a strong woman, a fighter who is not afraid of the emperor with his armies, nor the pope with his canonical concerns.

The first aspect characterizes two episodes which took place during the war that affected the valley of Spoleto, because of the raids perpetrated by the imperial armies fighting for Frederick II. Various testimonies of the Process of Canonization speak of it:

> She also said once, at the time of the war of Assisi, when certain Saracens scaled the wall and climbed down into the part within the cloister of St. Damian, where the

above-mentioned sisters were greatly afraid. But their most holy mother comforted them and scorned the forces of the invaders, saying: "You need not fear, for they cannot harm us". And, having spoken thus, she sought help in customary prayer. Such was the power of the oration that the Saracen enemies, without causing any injury, left as if driven out, in that they touched no one in the house. When asked how she knew these things, she said she had been present. (*Process, Testimony* 3; *sora Filippa di Leonardo di Gislerio*)

The "Saracen" mercenaries left, but the following year, in the summer of 1241, Vitalis di Aversa returned and besieged Assisi. It is Sister Francesca di Capitanio di Coldimezzo (relative through marriage of Jacopone da Todi) who provides us with key particulars, recalling how Clare, lying ill, called her sisters around her, inviting them to fast and pray, after having scattered ashes on her own and their heads. It is interesting to note the gratitude she shows for "her" Assisi, gratitude Clare expresses as she motivates the sisters to pray: "We have received much good from this city, and so we must pray to God to protect it" (*Process, Testimony* 9). This time, as well, the enemy withdraws and danger is avoided.

The second aspect concerns the difficulties Clare encountered within the Church, and the same Minor Order, difficulties in maintaining faith with the original experience that had inspired her to leave everything, and radically change her life.

But before speaking of this, I cannot avoid the issue of an alleged negligence attributed by someone on the part of Francis towards Clare and her companions, by having reduced his visits to St Damian, or for having established a kind of ritual distance to be understood as an emotional distancing from the

Pauperes Dominae (the Poor Sisters of St Damian), proof of which would be, for instance, his famous "silent sermon" before them, inside a circle of ashes that he had scattered around him. I do not believe that this episode is a sign of detachment. On the contrary, it is a further proof of a shared style, of a form of *imitatio Christi* and of dramatization, which Clare herself would in turn learn and imitate, when – as we have seen – she came forward in silence, and with ashes on her head, to face the soldiers who had violated the sanctity of the cloister.

I also feel, moreover, that it is a sign of "courtly" sensibility, the fact that Francis does not want to call Clare's companions "sisters" but "ladies," without seeing in this choice the malicious intention which a certain Friar Stefano found there, attributing to the *Poverello* a truly crude phrase against women (*Fonti Francescane* 2683).

It is also a distinguishing stylistic trait of Francis and Clare, that of wishing not to create a cult of themselves, but to always cleave to Christ, and this is much more important if seen in light of Francis's predilection for Clare. Besides, the Canticle of Brother Sun, written not by chance at St Damian, reminds us of this: the Creator is praised through ("by/for/with") his creatures, including the clear stars, that appear more lovable because we know their origin. And we must not forget that Francis, the minstrel of God, found other ways to be present, as for example in the composition of a song for Clare and her *Poverelle*, with melodies entrusted to the singing of his brothers, when illness, and prior to that, preaching, trips, the overseas mission, the drafting of rules, the relations with pontiffs, and coping with the improvement of the ever-growing Order all prevented him from seeing them in person. Clare was fully aware of this, and no words of disillusionment ever filter through her writings or actions towards Francis: this ability to love "from a distance" is, to my mind, one of the most convincing features of her personality.

On the other hand, Clare's relationship with the papacy and the Friars Minor, after Francis's death, appears decidedly problematic; this is a thematic context, which lends itself to the easy descent into disparate and radical assessments, which present her, on the one hand, as the overly sweet subservient saint, or, on the other, as a revolutionary feminist rebelling against the pope.

Two popes actually visited Clare at St Damian. The first meeting took place in July 1228, with Hugo of Ostia, once cardinal-protector of the Minor Order, and then pope, taking the name of Gregory IX. In previous years, he had favoured the foundation of female convents, which, although inspired by a "Franciscan" or "Clarian" tradition, he eventually directed towards traditional monastic forms, with the acceptance, for example, of property assets, thought to be indispensable in allowing women to lead a cloistered life, and to dedicate themselves to prayer. He had thus developed a *forma vitae* which he proposed to Clare, who accepted, on the condition of being able to safeguard the observance of absolute poverty for her community, with the utter refusal to receive goods, income, or lands.

Clare fervently declared to the pope: "Holy Father, I crave for absolution from my sins, but I desire not to be absolved from the obligation of following Jesus Christ."

Thus it was that the pontiff granted her the Privilege of Poverty, the so-called *Privilegium paupertatis* (in September 1228), extended as well to Sister Agnes, who had transferred to Perugia to the convent of Monteluce. In 1230, however, in answer to some members of the Order, who had consulted him on various questions, Gregory IX established, by means of the papal bull *Quo Elongati*, that only those friars holding the necessary apostolic licence could gain access into the female convents. Clare reacted intensely to the new disposition, and cast out from St Damian the Friars Minor who were residing there for the collection of alms and the liturgical service. She had, in fact, understood that, by submitting to papal approval, her convent, too, would be integrated into the other convents, which followed the above-mentioned rule of Cardinal Hugo. The pope, this time, as well, consented, and made an exception for St Damian. The conflict had brought to light the presence of misunderstandings between Clare and the Order of the Friars Minor, who obviously upheld the papal legal concerns, directed at bringing conformity to the female communities, and avoiding, among other things, the diffusion of penitential and assistance practices, such as those that had emerged among the sisters minor of Milan or Verona. Clare, however, found support in other parties, earlier companions of Francis (Philip, Angelo, and Leo), and, to the surprise of everyone (including some historians), she availed herself of the help of the much-discussed Brother Elias, the minister general from 1232 to 1239. The collaboration between the two can be verified both by a letter that Sister Agnes wrote, explicitly requesting that Elias be sent more often to comfort her community, and by the letters sent to another Agnes, daughter of the king of Bohemia, one of the most illustrious disciples of Clare. The fact itself that an epistolary exchange could take place between two such distant places is an obvious sign of collaboration provided to Clare from the highest of levels. But a more explicit reference demonstrates who was the main support to the drafting and delivery of the letters:

> In all of this, follow the example of our venerable Father, our Brother Elias, the Minister General, so that you may walk more securely in the way of the commands of the Lord. Prize it beyond the advice of others and cherish it as dearer to you than any gift. (*Second letter to Agnes of Prague*)

Elias was sharing with Clare a much bigger project, that of inviting Agnes of Prague to follow the practices of St Damian in her community, despite the contemporaneous and opposing pressure exerted on the princess by the pope. Learning of the correspondence, Gregory IX did not approve the initiative, nor did he forget when Elias, having fallen into disgrace and been removed from the position of minister, continued to visit several female convents: the pope excommunicated him. At this point, and not by chance, the correspondence between Prague and Assisi was also interrupted with the fourth and last letter that the abbess of St Damian wrote to Agnes just before she died.

Together with Elias, another dear friend of Francis, who was well-known for his role as secretary-writer, remained close to Clare: Brother Leo. The research of Attilio Bartoli Langeli has given us a wonderful and convincing discovery: the *Testament of Clare*, in a manuscript from Messina, is a document signed by Brother Leo, who inserted within it, among other things, a Benediction, according to the formula that he himself had received in a note (also signed) from Francis. Leo would also be present among the witnesses summoned to the Process of Canonization in 1253. Admitting to a collaboration between the two of them, even for the editing of Clare's writings, does not mean, however, that Leo imposed himself upon Clare's thoughts to change their substance. This further proof of friendship reinforces, if anything, the conviction that Clare of Assisi held in respect and esteem whomever she judged to be faithful to Francis's experience, beyond any logic of "alignment" internal or external to the Order.

But the difficulties continued with the new Pope Innocent IV (1243–54), who promulgated in 1247 a new normative text for the Order of St Damian, with a reference to the Rule of Francis only in relation to the three vows of personal poverty, chastity, and obedience. What a paradox to think that these convents going by the name of the Clarian community would follow any other lifestyle! This time, too, the Abbess of St Damian did not want to accept, and so she decided to write her own Rule with the help of the above-mentioned collaborators, and she demonstrated her steadfast position both to Cardinal Rinaldo of Ostia, sent by the pope to convince her, and to the pope himself who, a year later, went to see her. Following this meeting, Clare obtained the approval of her Rule, thus becoming the first woman founder of a religious Order in the history of the Church.

The Abbess of St Damian held in her hands on 9 August 1253, the day before her death, the solemn approval requested by her: "For you will sell this fatigue at a very high price and each one will be crowned queen in heaven with the Virgin Mary."

These words of Francis, read, heard, sung, and remembered, accompanied Clare's "fatigue" up until the last moment of her life, with a melody that remains unknown to this day, but one that we would so love to hear again.

CHAPTER SIX

BRIDGET

THE PILGRIM

Blonde, blue-eyed, and of regal origins: Bridget of Sweden has all the hallmarks of a fabled medieval heroine, like those who have made generations of little girls dream (this writer included).

She was born in a castle, and married in another castle, to the young man she loved. She was counsellor to the king and queen. She was cultured, refined, and studious. Besides her public figure, just the existence of Bridget has the flavour of adventure, given that, after having lived beneath the clear skies of the North, reflecting countless lakes or verdant forests, she left Scandinavia, crossing half of Europe, in order to encounter the more gentle and fleeting colours of Galician and Italian lands, to finally reach the bright horizons of Palestine. And in addition to the colours of the places, she was interested in the "colour of the souls" of women and men that she met, including kings, popes, and other princesses or wealthy ladies, together with many of the ordinary folk.

If however we immediately add her designation, which she deserved early on, namely that of "Saint," perhaps we risk veiling the dynamic, real, and profoundly feminine aspects of her life experience with a veneer of devotional formalism (or, conversely, of secular prejudice).

The challenge of these pages is to provisionally remove the halo from the Swedish prophetess, in order to try to discover just how much her story is one of an intense woman, and not of a stereotypical ideal.

Within a perspective which aspires to be realistic and not hagiographic in the rarefied sense of the term, what can help us is most recent historiography, which, with informed critical tools, has tackled for some time the medieval feminine mystique; as well as, in a completely different context, a literary work of incredible value, the most beautiful novel ever written on the European Middle Ages from the female point of view – the masterpiece by the Norwegian author Sigrid Undset, Nobel Prize winner for literature in 1928.

The story of Kristin Lavransdatter offers up some analogies with that of Bridget of Sweden, and introduces us, with pictorial efficacy, to the landscape and historical context of the Scandinavian Middle Ages, about which Sigrid's father – Ingvald Martin Undset – was an expert, due to his profession, that of archaeologist. The powerful descriptive realism of the novel, so different from the saccharine manner in which the Middle Ages was portrayed at the time, was what motivated the choice of this Norwegian writer as the recipient of the Nobel. Reading about Kristin we are granted a glimpse of Bridget's universe.

Set in the fourteenth century, Undset's novel begins with the protagonist's tranquil childhood, and then guides us through her turbulent youth and her falling in love with Erlend, to whom Kristin gives herself completely, breaking off her engagement to Simon, who also loves her with all of himself, to the extent that he later sacrifices his life to defend her honour. Jealousies and torments, however, mar Kristin's marriage. She gives birth to seven children, but she leaves Erlend, whom she too often compares to the radiant figure of her father. After being widowed, her sons grown, Kristin ultimately dons the habit of a pilgrim and reaches a convent, where she asks to be received, and where she eventually gives her life to save that of an innocent boy from the cruel superstition of some fanatics. In the background we have fourteenth-century Norway, with its dynastic struggles, with the popular beliefs in contrast to an as yet early Christian faith, with cities and small villages surrounded by a magnificent nature that Undset knows how to describe in an incomparable way, together with the most meticulous details of the domestic settings, of female fashion, or a peasant festival. Perhaps the extraordinary sensitivity of Sigrid Undset in weaving the story of Kristin, daughter of Lavrans, is also due to personal experiences, such as the premature death of a father, divorce from a husband, the care of three children, and a painful inner self-analysis that triggered a voyage through various countries, until in Italy, a country she especially loved, she converted to Catholicism. A serious intellectual, an early opponent to Nazism (and therefore in exile in New York), and a masterful artist, Undset is today little known, despite the enthusiastic homage paid to her in 1995 by another splendid Scandinavian woman, Liv Ullmann, who directed the film *Kristin Lavransdatter* based on the first part of the novel of the same name, maintaining the conviction of filming "the most beautiful story of love and passion ever written in the Norwegian language."

The same love, the same passion of Kristin, as told by Sigrid Undset, animated the life of Bridget: Birgitt Birgensdotter, daughter of the governor Birgen Persson and of the aristocratic Ingebord Bengsdotter, related through marriage to the royal house of Sweden.

Born in 1302 or 1303 in Finsta (around sixty kilometres northeast of Stockholm), Bridget lived until the age of eleven in her father's house. He was the governor of Uppland as well as counsellor to the sovereign. As proof of his prestige, the family had a burial chapel built in the Cathedral of Uppsala, where little Bridget is depicted in a bas-relief together with her brothers and sisters. After the death of her mother in 1314, in order to complete her education, the girl was sent, for two years, further south to nearby Lake Sommen, to the house of her godmother Karin Bensdotter and her husband, who was the administrator of that region, as well as a member of the council for the protection of the young King Magnus Eriksson. Bridget thus moved closer to the provinces of central-south Sweden, "dotted with blue lakes," where she would live for a long time: in Ulfåsa, as the wife of the knight Ulf Gudmarsson; in Alvastra and Vadstena – on Lake Vättern – as a "religious laywoman" who undertook, at around forty years of age, a more specific and unusual mission. Bridget also took from these places the name of "Princess of Nericia," a Latin term indicating the region of Närke, of which her husband became governor around 1330.

Bridget and Ulf celebrated their wedding in 1316, when she was fourteen (or fifteen) and he eighteen – the standard age for young newlyweds in the fourteenth century. On the whole the marriage was peaceful, if we believe the bride who described Ulf as "dear as his heart," and also fecund, given that from 1319 to 1334 eight children were born: Martha, Karl, Birger, Bengt, Gudmar, Karin, Ingeborg, and Cecilia. Bridget took care of her children's education, employing two in-house tutors for them, while the parents themselves broadened their own culture: for Bridget that meant an enrichment of her knowledge (especially of Latin), whereas for Ulf it meant starting almost from zero.

It was at this moment that a special meeting took place between the Lady of Ulfåsa and an important intellectual of the time: Canon Matthias of Linköping, a theological graduate who had studied in Paris, and who was the first to translate the Bible into Swedish (at the request, so it seems, of his aristocratic pupil). He expanded Bridget's horizons towards European culture. The literary and religious intellectual circle that was growing up around this married woman and her offspring became so well-known to the society of the time that King Magnus himself asked Bridget to move to the royal court to introduce Swedish customs to his own bride, Blanche of Namur. With this task, from 1336 to 1338, the future "prophetess of the North" had the chance to examine more closely the machinations of power. Despite the fact that she was chosen as godmother to the king's first-born, she was disappointed by too often being ignored, so Bridget returned to Ulfåsa. The other reason was to bury her little boy, Gudmar, who had died in the meantime.

Besides this sorrow, another profound sadness had already upset her family life, putting her in intense conflict with her husband. Bridget did not agree with Ulf in his choice of groom, a man she considered unworthy, for their first-born Martha. She suffered so much over this that she risked her health and that of her unborn child, who would be called Cecilia. This episode reveals that Bridget's marriage was not always as idyllic as one might have thought. Moments of adversity were followed by others of reconciliation. Seven years after their dispute, in 1341, the couple wished to celebrate their twenty-fifth anniversary with a long trip, one that was a kind of tradition in both their families – a trip that would take them across Europe all the way to Santiago de Compostela in faraway Galicia.

The pilgrimage's route crossed France in the midst of conflict with England – the Hundred Years War. The monstrous spectacle of two Christian sovereigns fighting each other deeply affected Bridget. Afterwards, in the sixth decade of that century, Bridget sent letters to the adversaries to invite them to consider peace. In this way, this most spirited woman began to formulate a plan for a political-religious commitment that would take her, in the second half of her life, way beyond the suggestiveness of the earth's edge found in Galicia.

In 1344, after twenty-eight years of marriage, Ulf Gudmarsson died, and his son Bengt followed suit shortly after. At the time of death, both were resident in the Cistercian monastery of Alvastra, where Bridget, too, had retired for a period of time, devoting herself to meditation and to preparation for what would soon become a more and more public and expanded mission. In the meantime, the widow divided her properties between the poor and her children: Karl stayed in Ulfåsa, taking over his father's role as administrator of Närke; Karin had in 1343 married Eggard von Kernen (much prized by his mother-in-law); Ingeborg was a nun in Riseberga; and little Cecilia was studying with the Dominicans in Skänninge, but without having any inclination towards consecrated life (as we will see). Bridget kept very little for herself of the substantial wealth she had inherited mostly from her father, because for a long time she had been fascinated with the Franciscan ideal, which she had already tried to follow during her marriage, associating herself with the tertiary members of the Order of Friars Minor together with her husband.

The Princess of Nericia stayed five more years in Sweden. She began to dictate those revelations which she was receiving in the form of visions to two secretary-confessors, Petrus Olavi of Alvastra and Petrus Olavi of Skänninge. Her fame as a mystic and prophetess quickly spread through the Nordic kingdom and, once again, King Magnus invited her to his court for advice, which was then distorted again (as in the case of an armed expedition against the Finlandians) or utterly disregarded. Bridget also dictated a short treatise on the good government of a Christian king, and asked Magnus (in vain) to offer to mediate in the enduring conflict between England and France.

As to the severity of the criticisms against her, due to general-ized bad manners, it is true that in Stockholm she was not spared either derision or hostility, as when dirty water was spilled onto her head from a window as she passed by, or when a male guest at court, during a banquet, approached her in a threatening manner and in a drunken state, and gave her to understand that prophecies were the business of priests and not of "pretty ladies." The meeting between her and a cleric – an encounter which seems to have taken place in a secluded forest – was actually dangerous. This was the man whom the king had appointed to collect the taxes. Bridget had pointed out to the cleric that he should have been thinking about matters of God and not those of Caesar. So the king fired the tax collector, who obviously did not appreciate this decision, and confronted her with violence and threats.

Ulf's widow was not the type of woman willing to go home quietly to spin wool in front of the fireplace. But she did not let this misunderstanding perturb her, and finally began to take interest in the "problem of problems" that was affecting Christi-anity at the time: the absence of the popes from Rome, after the moving of the papacy to Avignon. In the second half of the fourth decade in the fourteenth century, Bridget, still in Sweden, sent two messengers to the south of France with passionate and harsh letters, inviting Peter's successor to come back to Rome, until she personally decided to move to the Eternal City, stating to her friends that she had to obey an order from the Lord himself, who had promised her that in Rome she would again meet the pope and the emperor.

Before leaving for Italy, the "Swedish Sybil" achieved a bless-ing in disguise: the sovereigns Magnus and Blanche granted her the royal castle of Vadstena (on Lake Vättern). The place was truly charming and ideal for what Bridget had been planning for some time with her collaborators: the foundation of a double monastic Order – a female convent, next to a house of priests, who would however obey the abbess, according to the analogous model of Fontevrault and other places. Despite the fact that she continued to be a laywoman, a Franciscan tertiary, and a Cistercian sympathizer, Bridget was seeking something different, and so she wrote a specific Rule for the new monastic Order, which she wished to have dedicated to the Most Holy Saviour; but the harsh letters that she had, in the meantime, sent to the Avignon pontiffs certainly did not foster papal approval. In fact it only officially arrived in 1378, five years after her death.

Bridget left Sweden in 1349. She crossed a Europe devastated by the plague and arrived in Rome in 1350, during the Jubilee. Thus she began the second period of her life in Italy, dedicating herself entirely to study and to the struggle for Church reform.

At first her secretaries and a few friends followed her; afterwards she was even joined by her daughter Catherine (Karin), who became one of her mother's principal collaborators. The group of Swedes was hosted in the palace of Cardinal Hugues de Beaufort and, on his return from Avignon, the group was received in the house of Francesca Papazurri, an extremely faithful friend and supporter of Bridget up until her death. The house of Francesca Papazurri was located where, to this day, we find the Church of Santa Brigida in the Piazza Farnese. This Roman lady was prepared to host the Scandinavian pilgrims who reached the city of the Apostle Peter, and who, in her home, found lodging or guidance, besides the opportunity to confess in their own language. There was a curious episode in which a Finnish pilgrim could not make himself understood in confession with Petrus of Skänninge, who, disconsolate over not being able to communicate, sought out Bridget for assistance in the matter.

To anyone asking what she was doing in Rome, Bridget replied that she was praying, writing, and studying Latin. This universal language of Western Christians was, in fact, considered essential to her in her endeavour to renew the Church and the society of her time, even through a form of true feminine preaching, which she later experimented with in Naples and Cyprus. In order to improve the Latin version of the texts she continued to dictate in the Swedish language, Bridget also added Alfonso Pecha de Vadaterra to her first cohort of secretaries. He made a fundamental contribution to the compilation of the complete body of Bridget's works that have come down to us: the *Revelationes* (Revelations), which he separated into eight books; a series of *Revelationes extravagantes* (Supplementary Revelations); the monastic Rule; and some minor writings. Alfonso came from Andalusia, where he was the Bishop of Jaén. Having joined the Swedish group in Rome, he proceeded to accompany Bridget during the pilgrimage to Jerusalem (of which we will speak later on). And afterwards, he remained committed, along with Catherine, in both the phase of the Process of Canonization for her mother, and for the recognition of the Brigidine Order.

Andalusia and Sweden: two very different and distant lands. Also distant in time had been the conversion to Christianity of both these peoples, the Iberian one taking place in late Antiquity, that of Sweden flowering in the early twelfth century (1108). And yet, the differences notwithstanding, the Andalusian Bishop Alfonso put himself entirely at the disposal of Bridget of Sweden (who was moreover a laywoman) and he did it when her fame as a "visionary mystic" was still controversial.

Bridget in Rome was not spared the lack of understanding and the hostility towards her, in part due to her criticism of the conduct of many monks. During an outing to the monastery of Farfa, for instance, this prestigious visitor did not hesitate to call those monks living an immoral life "animals." They had not even received her in the guesthouse but rather in a sort of "storage closet." The Scandinavian princess was also disliked by certain Roman citizens, who were obviously taking advantage of the climate of anarchy to further their own interests, and therefore had no appetite for any type of reform. Someone, moreover, accused Bridget of being allied with the House of Orsini, given that a young representative of that noble house had courted Catherine, who had recently become widowed, but was still beautiful and young. The marriage proposal was rejected, but the gossip went on unabated, and these people, who considered the foreign noblewoman a bearer of ill-fortune, were not appeased. A group of thugs even tried to storm the palace in which Bridget was staying, but the ugly episode ended with merely some broken windows, and a failed attempt to break down the front door.

Bad news in the meantime arrived from the political and ecclesiastical fronts, as neither Emperor Charles IV of Bohemia nor the pope, when contacted in writing by the Swedish visionary, deemed her worthy of response. Even though Bridget continued to pray for Pope Clement VI, she exposed the most serious of his errors, using cutting descriptions: "His body is full of worms, his arms are two snakes, and in his heart lurks a scorpion" (*Revelationes*, I, 28). One wonders how such a daring woman could go unpunished! But Bridget was not afraid, nor did she ever abandon her intent to reform.

In the meantime, some of her distant children were causing her anxiety: with the help of her brother Charles, Cecilia, the last child, the one who had almost died in her mother's womb, had escaped the convent. After some initial displeasure, Bridget accepted Cecilia's marriage because she had been told in a vision: "The daughter you have offered me is like a vine. And since I know that for her there exists a more favourable terrain, I will plant her there. You must not grieve for having given her your consent" (*Revelationes*, IV, 71). After all, so this visionary recalls, God appreciated three women who lived very different circumstances: Susanna, Judith, and St Thecla; the first was married, the second a widow, and the third a virgin. This passage of the

Revelations is important for understanding how Bridget of Sweden had a more positive vision of marriage than some of her hagiographers wanted us to believe.

Cecilia married twice, and called a daughter Bridget, who then took the veil in Vadstena, the convent founded by her grandmother.

The Swedish political situation was also in turmoil. Birger Ulfsson, who arrived in Rome in 1355 to visit his mother and sister, brought bad news of intrigues, rebellions, and wars, which caused the excommunication of King Magnus (1358), the loss of the province of Scania to Denmark (1360), and the ascent of the young Albrecht of Magdeburg (1364) to the Swedish throne. Queen Blanche of Namur had died in the meantime in 1363.

This was not a good epilogue for those who had been, at one time, two young and promising sovereigns, whose wedding the Lady of Ulfåsa had attended, bringing the gift of a Holy Bible and later helping them with her precious but unheeded advice. But – as we all know – it is often the destiny of prophetesses to be ignored ...

This misunderstanding, however, did not impede Bridget's fervour. She devoted herself to pilgrimages on Italian soil, visiting Assisi, Naples, Salerno, Bari, and San Michele al Gargano. Wherever she went, Bridget carefully chose stops near the tombs of saints; she met all kinds of people and left some mark (often lasting) of her presence. This had already happened on previous stages of her journey in Italy, as she descended from the north, along the way towards Rome: in Milan, for instance, where she had urged Archbishop Giovanni Visconti to not gloat over his worldly power.

Bridget's visit in 1365 to Naples had important political and personal consequences: the Swedish noblewoman made a surprising bond of friendship with Queen Joanna I of Anjou, to the extent that she decided to stop for two years in the Parthenopean city, where she would return in 1372, on her way to Jerusalem, and in 1373 on her way back.

Bridget the prophetess and Joanna the queen: in appearance two women poles apart, and yet their relationship constitutes a very interesting and emblematic facet of those intensely human characteristics in the personality of the Swedish saint. As such, it is necessary to linger a while longer on this relationship.

Joanna was born in 1325, and when only seventeen, she became queen of Naples and Countess of Provence, having ascended the Angevin throne in the absence of legitimate male heirs. Despite the fact that her grandfather, Robert of Anjou, had meticulously prepared her succession, aware of the risks involved with her being an underage woman, her long reign (1343–82) was characterized by continuous and bloody struggles for power. In particular, her opposition came from the Hungarian branch of the Angevins, and the second-born branches of Taranto and Durazzo. After the assassination of her first consort, Joanna was accused of having commissioned the murder, but she managed to get exonerated; she contracted marriages with three other men, who, one after the other, died, without putting an end to the anarchy, to the confusion, or to the crimes. Only the fourth husband, Otto, the Duke of Brunswick, was of some help in her last military contests, which, even so, ended badly for her: shortly after the Great Schism of the Church, preferring to support Clement VII instead of the Neapolitan Urban VI, the queen found herself isolated and defenceless. Joanna was killed at age fifty-seven, suffocated in her bed, on the order of her nephew Charles of Durazzo, who, around twenty years before, had been saved, thanks to her, from a death sentence.

Bridget of Sweden and her friends met the queen of Naples in a moment of relative calm. The period from 1366 to 1378 was indeed the most auspicious, not only for Joanna but also for her whole domain, in the almost forty years of her reign. During their first encounter, the Swedes obtained from the queen the safe-conduct documents to travel to the sanctuaries of Apulia, as well as financial support, in view of a pilgrimage that was particularly dangerous, given the presence of mercenaries and bandits in the turbulent southern zones of her kingdom. On her return from Gargano, Bridget rested at the royal residence of Aversa, where she was also received in 1372 together with her three children – Karl, Birger, and Karin. It was love at first sight for Bridget's eldest son, and within a few weeks he became the queen's lover, despite the complication of a Swedish wife left at home. The relationship, as passionate as it was illegitimate, did not last long because Karl suddenly fell ill (perhaps the plague), and he died in March of 1372, precisely when the Swedish party was about to set sail for the Holy Land.

Notwithstanding the pain of loss over her "Son of Tears" (*Revelationes*, VII, 13), Bridget did not hold a grudge against the passionate sovereign. Reassured by a vision of the salvation of Karl's soul, Bridget brought back from Jerusalem a small gold cross for Joanna, which the queen cherished as a keepsake. However, the prophetess of the North warned Joanna and the nobility of the kingdom against certain serious evils that she had noticed in Naples, and which she denounced in a sermon, written in Latin, that she had read in her presence by her secretary-confesssor Alfonso before the prominent citizens of the city. First of all, Bridget said that it was a scandal to witness the slave trade in a Christian country, and she also pointed out the widespread custom of resorting to witches and soothsayers. She took offence at the ostentatious lavishness of the clothing then in vogue among the aristocratic and wealthy Neapolitans.

The harshness of her admonitions should not detract from the reality that Bridget's visit to Naples was seen as a light of hope in the midst of continuous hardships, in a city governed by a rationale of power that was totally opposed to the Christian ideal. This rationale was so entrenched as to give the idea that there was no possibility of transformation. And yet, during her Neapolitan sojourn, Bridget managed to even reconcile the two rival families of Di Costanzo and Mormile, who had been violently at war for a decade.

The controversial figure of Joanna I of Anjou also found in Bridget of Sweden a guide, whom the sovereign tried to follow, as much as her temperament and the cruel political climate permitted her. We know that Joanna, before her death, was one of the chief supporters of the canonization of the Swedish saint. Bridget perhaps also left her mark on the artistic patronage of Queen Joanna: the theme of the Passion, so dear to this Swedish mystic, is actually at the centre of the pictorial cycle of the Church of Santa Maria Incoronata of Naples, founded by the Angevin sovereign, between 1370 and 1380.

Now we must take a deeper look at the mystic revelations of Bridget. We will start with those that the celebrated pilgrim dictated mostly towards the end of her life, even in Jerusalem itself, during her final challenging voyage, undertaken between March of 1372 and February of 1373 in the Holy Land.

Together with other medieval mystics, Bridget of Sweden identified and developed the theme of compassion for God. Beyond identifying totally with the suffering of Christ on the cross, Bridget dwells, in particular, on the specific human and emotional aspects of the relationship between the Madonna and her Son. As regards the presence of the Mother beneath the cross, some elements of Bridget's depiction are directly in tune with those that would be expressed in Charles Péguy, centuries later.

Through Bridget, Mary tells the story of her maternal sorrow:

After that they put the crown of thorns on his head and
it cut so deeply into my Son's venerable head that the
blood filled his eyes as it flowed, blocked up his ears and

stained his beard as it ran down. As he stood on the cross
wounded and bloody, he felt compassion for me who was
standing by in tears and, looking with his bloodied eyes
in the direction of John, my nephew, he commended me
to him. At the time I could hear some people saying that
my Son was a thief, others that he was a liar, still others
that no one was more deserving of death than my Son.
My sorrow was renewed from hearing all this. But, as I
said before, when the first nail was driven into him, that
first blow shook me so much that I fell down as if dead,
my eyes covered in darkness, my hands trembling, my
feet unsteady. In the bitterness of my grief I was not able
to watch until he had been fastened entirely to the cross.
When I got up, I saw my Son hanging there in misery and,
in my thorough dismay, I his most unhappy Mother, could
hardly stand on my feet due to grief … Then, out of the
exceeding bodily anguish of his human nature, he cried
out to the Father: 'Father, into your hands I commend my
spirit.' When I his most sorrowful Mother, heard those
words, my whole body shook with the bitter pain of my
heart. As often as I have thought on that cry since then, it
has still remained present and fresh in my ears … Then he
was taken down from the cross. I took his body on my lap;
it was like a leper's, all livid. His eyes were lifeless and full
of blood, his mouth as cold as ice, his beard like twine, his
face grown stiff. His hands had become so rigid that they
could not be bent farther down than to about his naval.
I had him on my knee just as he had been on the cross,
like a man stiff in all his limbs. After that they laid him in
a clean linen and with my linen cloth I dried his wounds
and his limbs and then closed his eyes and mouth, which
had been opened when he died. Then they placed him in
the sepulchre. How I would rather have been placed in

there alive with my Son, if it had been his will! These
things done, dear John came and brought me to his
house. See, then, my daughter, what my Son has endured
for you! (*Revelationes*, VI, 57–8)

The Passion is memorialized by Bridget with a sense of identification so truly poignant as to make us better understand the
feelings of Mary.

When our mystic asked the Madonna what had happened after
the death of Jesus, she responds in this way: "I did what I had to
do, and I moved among my own kind like any other person. But
a few years after my Son's death, I longed to see him again" (*Revelationes*, VI, 60). How could one not feel in this passage an echo
of the longing that Bridget herself experienced at having already
seen three of her children die in that moment in which she was
dictating the content of her visions?

The two women – the Mother and her daughter in spirit –
achieved such a sense of mutual familiarity as to be able to even
linger on intimate specifics, such as when Mary recounted her
virginal birth and when she gently tended to her Child, swaddling
him in linen and then woollen cloths (this Brigidine representation also had an influence on some late medieval iconographic
models portraying the Nativity). Another example of an intimate detail is when she felt a legitimate pleasure in describing the
beauty of that Son, who, in the meantime, had become great
(thus revealing to us Bridget's ideal of masculine beauty):

He was tall for the men of medium height in those days,
not fleshy but well-built as to muscles and bones. His
hair, eyelashes, and beard were golden-brown. His beard
was a palm-width in length. His forehead was neither
prominent nor sunken, but straight. His nose was evenly

built neither too little nor too large. His eyes were so limpid that even his enemies loved to gaze on him. His lips were not too thick and were bright red. His jaw did not jut out and was not too long but attractive and of a fine length. His cheeks were nicely rounded. He was fair-skinned with traces of red and he had a straight posture. There was not a blemish on his whole body, as his scourgers can testify who saw him bound to the pillar completely naked. My son possessed such a gift of beauty that those who looked on him used to be comforted from whatever sorrow was in their hearts. (*Revelationes*, I)

All mothers desire beauty for their children and advise each other on how they can maintain it. This concern goes as far as re-adjusting a crooked collar or cleaning the stains from a shirt, time after time. This is why Mary, years before, had reproached Bridget because she was too intent on her religious devotions, while allowing her daughter Catherine to go around in a dishevelled manner. Exactly like that! After having presented to the Madonna a new prayer that she had composed, the Swedish prophet heard this admonition from the heavenly Mother: "Think rather to the sewing of your daughter's garment. What she is wearing is not a skirt of silk but of rough wool, more-over it is old and patched!" (*Revelationes extravagantes*, 69)

These words help us understand how Bridget of Sweden had always been first and foremost a mother: not only during her youth spent in the distant land of Sweden where she had given birth and ministered to her offspring, but also afterwards, in other places and in other ways. Her multiple activities are all tinged with this sense of motherhood: her activities as a mystic, a prophetess, a political counsellor, a religious reformer, and a simple friend or spiritual guide over her long life that, in 1373, was coming to its end.

The exertions of the voyage across the sea, in itself already demanding for a woman of almost seventy, were complicated due to the fact that Bridget in Cyprus, on her way home, engaged once again in a vain attempt at political-religious pacification, preaching in Latin before the people and Queen Eleanor of Aragon. She did so as well, as we have seen, in Naples, and, having reached Rome, dictated again a long letter for Gregory XI, sending this time her trusted Andalusion secretary-confessor as her messenger to Avignon. He didn't arrive in time to see her alive on his return; nor was the prophetess of the North able to see the pope come back to Rome. He was persuaded to leave Avignon by another woman, so different from Bridget, and yet, at the same time, so similar – Catherine of Siena.

Bridget of Sweden died 23 July 1373, in the Roman house of Francesca Papazurri.

It seems that this Italian friend may have stated that she never stopped missing Bridget from the moment the blue eyes of her guest deserted her.

CHAPTER SEVEN

CHRISTINE

THE WRITER

One day, I was sitting in my study surrounded by many books of different kinds, for it has long been my habit to engage in the pursuit of knowledge. My mind had grown weary as I had spent the day struggling with the weighty tomes of various authors whom I had been studying for some time, I looked up from my book and decided that, for once, I would put aside these difficult texts and find instead something amusing and easy to read from the works of the poets. As I searched around for some little book, I happened to chance upon a work which did not belong to me but was amongst a pile of others that had been placed in my safe-keeping. I opened it up ... Yet I had scarcely begun to read it when my dear mother called me down to supper, for it was time to eat. I put the book to one side resolving to go back to it the following day.

These words could describe a common experience of some intellectual living today, who, after hours of demanding study, decides to take it easy with some lighter reading. From the above-quoted passage, we can infer that the writer is lucky enough to own a house with a study, with a wealth of reading material (some volumes scattered about), and to be living with a mother who cooks for her. Furthermore, it is understood that the author of the text is a woman, who studies for professional reasons ("for it has long been my habit to engage in the pursuit of knowledge").

If however we date this record, and we learn the identity of who said it, perhaps it would startle us to find out that the intellectual in question is a forty-year-old widow who supports herself, her three children, her mother, and a niece by means of her writing, in Paris, in the year 1405. Our writer is, in fact, one of the bravest and most intelligent women that the waning Middle Ages has yielded to history: Christine de Pizan, born in Venice in 1365, but who lived in France from the tender age of four.

Christine's family was originally from Pizzano, a town just outside Bologna, in whose university her father, Tommaso, completed studies in medicine and astrology. Once in service to the state of Venice, Tommaso da Pizzano married in the city on the lagoon, and had three children: Christine, Paolo, and Aghinolfo. After having received prestigious invitations to serve the monarchs of France or Hungary, because of his widespread fame as a man of culture, Tommaso chose the French King Charles V, called the Wise, and the family moved to Paris in 1369, when his first-born was only four. A tranquil childhood at court gave the young girl a comfortable life and a robust cultural education, thanks to her father's teachings and free access to the royal library.

In 1380 Christine married a gentleman of twenty-four from Picardy, Etienne de Castel. Theirs was an extraordinarily happy marriage, but in September of the same year, a storm threatened the serenity of the fifteen-year-old bride because the "Wise" king and the fortunes of the Pizzano family fell rapidly into decline. During the next ten years, Christine lost her father (1387) and her husband (1390), finding herself alone to support her family, to fight to recuperate her paternal estate in the Chambre des Comptes (Court of Auditors) in Paris, because it was contested (she would win, but the trial lasted fifteen years!), and ultimately, to fight the sadness that oppressed her. The poem *Seulette sui* expresses so well her sorrow: "Alone am I and alone I wish to be, / Alone my gentle friend has left me." Christine felt alone and the times were not peaceful, because the political situation already presaged the civil war that would bring bloodshed to France in the decades to come. And yet, at only twenty-eight years of age, the young widow made the voluntary and steadfast choice to never remarry, so great was her love for Etienne. This was not easy for such a passionate woman, who would write, after fifteen years of widowhood: "There is no stronger or closer bond in the world, than that which Nature, in accordance with God's wishes, creates between man and woman" (*The Book of the City of Ladies*, 1, 8).

After having lived through substantial impoverishment over the course of four years, Christine recovers, and understands that her literary knowledge could become a means to "being reborn." Thus, in 1394, her career as a writer begins. She sends poems to friends who stayed on at the royal court, and immediately achieves success with some illustrious clients, such as the two brothers of Charles V (the Dukes of Berry and Bourgogne), Queen Isabella of Bavaria, the Duke of Orléans, and his wife, Valentina Visconti.

In the first six years of work, this poet writes sixteen books and establishes a scriptorium (today we would say a small publishing house), in which the manuscripts are copied, finely illuminated (we know the name of one of her collaborators, an expert in the art of the miniature: Anastasia), and sometimes signed by Christine, who keeps her father's surname. During this phase, what Christine produces exclusively reflects courtly poetry, with its well-established genres such as the ballad, and with references to personal and amorous subject matter. Her success is such that the writer receives (just as happened at one time to her father!) an invitation from the English king to move to England, and one from Gian Galeazzo Visconti to return to Italy, to Milan; but her desire to stay in Paris prevails over every offer of a financial nature. Actually, the renewed sense of well-being allows her to deepen her knowledge of the classics, of other medieval writers, and of several Italian authors, including Dante and Boccaccio. It was, in fact, Christine who would contribute to the diffusion of the Divine Comedy in France.

At this point, something truly extraordinary takes place in the life of this courageous woman: the public dispute regarding the *Roman de la Rose* (more specifically its second part, written by Jean de Meun), a dispute launched by Christine against certain exponents of the Parisian university milieu. This book was enjoying great success, but according to Christine, it constituted a betrayal of the chivalric values, and represented a threat against true love, something which she, herself, had experienced with Etienne, and which had given her the means to articulate a genuine feminine dignity.

It was no easy thing to get involved in a discussion with academia, whose representatives presumed that they were the official and exclusive custodians of culture, but Christine was not to be intimidated. By 1399, in another document of hers, she had denounced the obtuse and vulgar intellectualism of Jean de Meun, who stated that women did not have any virtue, and therefore were nothing more than an object of instinctive pleasure for the "learned male." The debate on the *Roman de la Rose* occupied Christine for the entire year of 1402, and it reveals her intellectual and moral sensitivity towards issues regarding not only literature, but also the society and customs of her time.

The controversy created a scandal between academics, who constituted a powerful and elitist caste. Her chief adversaries were Gontier Col and Jean de Montreuil, with whom she initiated a confrontational exchange of letters. But from the same Parisian university milieu arose a most authoritative voice, who gave credence to the challenger – Jean Gerson, who would compose a brief treatise supporting the view in opposition to the

Roman de la Rose, and who would give many public lectures on the subject. Other prestigious personalities stand with Christine: the provost of Paris, Guillaume de Tignonville, and Marshall Boucicaut, founder of the chivalric Order of the "Green Shield with the White Lady." In the meantime, our polemicist also takes the initiative to dedicate to the queen a collection of letters related to the debate on the *Roman de la Rose*, and to work on behalf of reconvening the ancient Courts of Love, like those that existed in the time of Eleanor of Aquitaine. She manages as well to reunite her supporters in the house of the Duke of Orléans, as the debate sweeps throughout Paris. The last word on the subject would be from Christine, who writes a letter to Pierre Col (Gontier's brother): "You claim to have cured a friend of yours of love-sickness, by making him read the *Roman de la Rose*: Who is not going to believe that you would have cured him better, by making him read the writings of St. Bernard?" And again: "Many have faithfully loved ... and through this love became courageous and much esteemed, to the extent that in their old age they praised and thanked God for having been in love" (these are words that express an authentic religiosity and therefore we will review them later). The letter ends with an ironic remark: "For my part, I do not intend to write any more about the matter, whoever may write to me, for I have not undertaken to drink the entire Seine. Your devoted friend of science, Christine de Pizan."

After this dispute, our author's interests are decidedly directed towards history, philosophy, and politics: Christine's mind is so dynamic and open that she is able to recognize not only cultural transformations, but also disturbing political divisions, destabilizing the kingdom of France, easy prey to internal and external enemies.

Her most important historic work of this period is a treatise in prose on the ideal sovereign (*Livre des faits et bonnes moeurs du sage roi Charles V*), which had been commissioned by Philip the Bold,

Duke of Burgundy, who would however die before the book was finished, and would leave behind an even more unsettled political situation. Besides writing two hefty volumes of an allegorical and moral nature (*Epistre d'Othea a Hector; Livre du chemin de long estude*), and the already mentioned *Book of the City of Ladies* (*Cité des Dames*), Christine's principal preoccupation, over a period of seven years, would be to try to preserve the peace, in the midst of the growing violence surrounding her. To this effect, she wrote two moving letters to Queen Isabella in 1405 and in 1410, when open war was declared between the Armagnac faction and the Burgundian faction. Books such as the *Livre des faits d'armes et de chevalerie* and the *Livre de la paix* demonstrate how vigorous was Christine's struggle for peace: if absolutely necessary, war – she explains – has rules that must be followed, such as the respect for civilian populations and prisoners, and the absolute refusal to engage in pillaging and indiscriminate massacres. Christine perseveres, and contacts anyone who could intervene, but all her efforts are in vain. The situation worsens. The fact that she stops writing to the powers-that-be, however, does not represent a departure from her political commitment. During these painful years, she turns to the writing of a meditation on the Passion of Christ. When Paris is taken by the Burgundians, she leaves the city and withdraws (most probably) to the convent of Poissy, where her daughter was living, along with many other French aristocratic women. From 1418, for almost a decade, silence engulfs the life of Christine until her fervour is reawakened, in celebration of the ventures of Joan of Arc, who had managed to liberate Orléans from siege (8 May 1429) and get King Charles VII crowned in Reims:

Oh! What honour for the feminine sex! God has shown his regard for it, in contrast to all the people who

destroyed the Kingdom and ran away and quit. Now
recovered and saved by a woman, who did what 5,000
men could not, and now the traitors are no more ...
Blessed is He who created you Joan, born at a most
portentous time!

Thus writes Christine in July of 1429. She has regained all the
strength and enthusiasm of her youth in the composition of her
last work, that *Ditié de Jehanne d'Arc*, which expresses all the redis-
covered consolation in seeing the two great ideals of her own life
fulfilled in the Maid of Orléans: feminine dignity and the pursuit of peace. Would Christine have known that her friend Jean
Gerson had already composed, two months before her, a treatise
honouring Joan? It would seem so; the war had separated her
from her old ally, but the two of them, even from a distance,
embraced the same emotions, and knew how to recognize the
signs of the times.

Some others, however, in the usual Parisian milieu of the
university academics, at the time supporters of the English,
acted differently, and were already weaving a plot against the
Maid of Orléans: among these detractors is Pierre Cauchon, the
rector of the university, who would become Joan's chief accuser
at the infamous trial in Rouen. In some parts of her *Ditié* (Song),
Christine foresees the danger and warns: "Oh! All you blind
people, can you not see in this God's hand? Do you really want
to fight against Him?" Towards the end of this vibrant poem, her
reference is even more explicit: "I don't know if Paris will hold
out, (For they have not reached there yet), or if the Maid will
delay if they resist." Even in the exaltation of the moment, the
writer, who knows how to compose poetry and political tracts,
shows that she has not lost her surprising lucidity and strong
practical spirit, right up until the very end. She would certainly

have wished to counsel the Maid, if she could have, but these two great women (both warriors in their own way) did not meet, and Christine would be spared the suffering of seeing Joan's martyrdom, because her own death would take place before that terrible day in May 1431.

Retracing, although briefly, the life of Christine, we see already proof of the incomparable value of her personality (in this light, it is recommended that one read her letters and her autobiography, *L'Avision de Christine*); but the immensity and complexity of her literary output would entail further detailed study beyond the scope of this book. At the very least, however, we can offer here some small suggestion of a recurring interpretation of her philosophy, even though it does not entirely do her justice.

The words quoted at the beginning of this chapter belong to the introduction to her most famous book, *The Book of the City of Ladies*, and they mention the almost casual discovery of a slight volume which contains shameful accusations against women, and which prompts Christine to write a tract in defence of herself and the female sex. The work had widespread success early on and was translated into other languages in the fifteenth century. It is preserved in magnificent illuminated manuscripts in the Bibliothèque Nationale de France, and studied by numerous scholars (especially within the Francophone and Anglo-American communities). It has finally been made accessible in the Italian language (at the late date of 1997) thanks to the beautiful and commendable edition edited by Patrizia Caraffi and Earl Jeffrey Richards. (A new English edition was translated, introduced, and annotated by Rosalind Brown-Grant in 1999 and it is quoted here.)

The Book of the City of Ladies is therefore enjoying – and rightly so – good fortune with translations in diverse languages. The interest of many author/scholars, focussing on this text, risks however disregarding other themes to which Christine, a prolific writer in various sectors of learning, devoted her intellectual and civic attention.

I also believe that the extraordinary service she rendered to women must be investigated, by reflecting, in a more general way, on the roots of her education, all the while being careful not to apply modern interpretive criteria to her time. Christine de Pizan truly defended feminine dignity, but she did it on the basis of the three cultural nuclei that the era in which she lived could offer up to her: the courtly mentality, pre-humanistic culture, and Christian religiosity.

While the first is evident in the already quoted controversy on the *Roman de la Rose*, the second influences the very structure of the *Book of the City of Ladies*, a work that wishes, by using a "book," to create a "city," in which women may be able to defy misogynistic beliefs, and recover models of proven feminine virtue, by means of the heroines of Antiquity, Christian saints, and literary personages, presented by three allegorical figures: Reason, Rectitude, and Justice. Besides the obvious Augustinian model of the City of God, a literary source for the work would be the *De mulieribus claris* by Boccaccio, who, however, had stated that he could not cite women of his own era because it was difficult to find virtuous ones. Christine obviously disagrees, and speaks of medieval women (even if she could not have possibly been acquainted with the whole of the female culture that preceded her!). Her humanism possesses a totally personal articulation of its own, and it is expressed with brash originality, in connection with her classical literary preferences. Thus Virgil is set above Ovid in a dialogue between the author and Reason:

> My lady, why is it that Ovid, who is considered to be the greatest of poets (though others, myself included, think that Virgil is more worthy of that accolade, if you don't mind my saying so), made so many derogatory remarks

about women in his writings, such as the *Art of Love*, the *Remedies of Love*, and other works? (*The Book of the City of Ladies*, 1, 9)

The answer is like a short sermon that could have been given by Jean Gerson during the *Roman de la Rose* controversy:

> Ovid was a man very well versed in the theory and practice
> of writing poetry and his fine mind allowed him to excel
> in everything he wrote. However, his body was given over
> to all kinds of worldliness and vices of the flesh: he had
> affairs with many women, since he had no sense of mod-
> eration and showed no loyalty to any particular one.
> (*The Book of the City of Ladies*, 1, 9)

The third cultural foundation, Christianity, is apparent in the whole of Christine's oeuvre. Furthermore she was probably very influenced by the mindset pervading the Late Middle Ages about which Johan Huizinga reminded us: the *Devotio moderna* (Modern Devotion). We must not forget that the main text of this movement, *The Imitation of Christ*, was attributed by some scholars not to Thomas à Kempis, but to Christine's dear friend, Jean Gerson. At any rate, in Christine, this sensitivity towards the *devotio* emerges with particular enthusiasm in her commentary on certain passages from the Holy Scripture, with respect to which she exhibits not only a thorough exegetical competence, but also that personal and profound capacity of identification with the biblical text. In reference to the creation of woman, an obviously central theme in the debate on feminine dignity, Christine comments on the first chapter of the Book of Genesis in these terms:

> God endowed both male and female with this soul, which
> He made equally noble and virtuous in the two sexes.

Whilst we're still on the subject of how the human body was framed, woman was created by the very finest of craftsmen. And where exactly was she made? Why, in the earthly paradise. What from? Was it from coarse matter? No, it was from the finest material that had yet been invented by God: from the body of man himself. (*The Book of the City of Ladies*, I, 9)

This interpretation was already circulating among many medieval commentators, as Marie-Thérèse d'Alverny has shown us in her masterful study. But Christine adds a deeper dimension, when she identifies a "parity in diversity" between men and women:

So God created man and woman to serve Him in different ways and to help and comfort one another, according to a similar division of labour. To this end, He endowed each sex with the qualities and attributes which they need to perform the tasks for which they are cut out. (*The Book of the City of Ladies*, I, II)

This balanced view is not only the result of intellectual reflection, but is also born, in my opinion, out of personal experience, and an intense serenity attained on an emotional level. Besides that previously discussed love for her husband, the positive relationship with her parents must have influenced this writer's mentality: if it is true, in fact, that in a passage from *The Book of the City of Ladies* (II, 36) Christine alludes to her father's encouragement towards her studies in contrast with her mother's preference for an emphasis on domestic chores (her needle and thread), elsewhere she does recall that, in her childhood, it was her mother who enveloped her in affection, thanks to which she grew up feeling deeply loved.

This emotional aspect gracefully comes to light in certain comments on evangelical episodes, in which women meet each other. In order to respond, for example, to those who believed that the female inclination to shed tears might be considered a sign of weakness, Christine reminds us of the tears of compassion shed by Jesus when he saw the sisters of Lazarus crying, and she adds:

> Nor did God scorn the tears of the widow who wept for her only son as he was being laid in the ground. When Christ saw her weeping, his compassion gushed forth like a fountain of mercy at the sight of her tears. Asking her, "Woman why are you crying?," he straightaway brought back her child from the dead. (*The Book of the City of Ladies*, I, 10)

The capacity for identification is also facilitated in this case by the fact that a child of Christine predeceased her, but, generally speaking, what affects us is the depth of her commentary on these evangelical episodes, in terms that are neither abstract nor conventional.

A final element to consider is the centrality of the Madonna in the redefinition of womanly dignity, at which this writer wishes to arrive. Triumphantly received in the City of Ladies, the Virgin Mother is depicted in procession with a book in hand (in the illuminated manuscript Harley 4431); this iconographic model cannot merely be interpreted in symbolic terms, as if Mary had become the disincarnate representation of wisdom or knowledge. Precisely at the end of her book, Justice invites the Madonna to enter the City, and although the author is well-pleased to have built a city in which women would be able to find refuge from their enemies, Christine warns the citizens not to feel superior because of this advantage they have received, but to follow "the example of your queen, the noble Virgin. On hearing that she was to receive the supreme honour of becom[ing] the mother of the Son of God, her humility grew all the greater as she offered herself up to the Lord as his handmaiden" (*The Book of the City of Ladies*, III, 19). There is nothing pietistic in this caution. If anything, certain paradoxes are recognized (grandeur/humility; weakness/strength), ones typical of that particular cultural context, together with the awareness on the part of Christine that Mary represented the most effective argument against misogynists of every race and gender. God did not scorn the womb of a woman, and within it he became incarnate.

The cultivated, learned, passionate, courageous Christine de Pizan had so profoundly understood the extraordinary novelty of this message as to make it the foundation of "her city."

CHAPTER EIGHT

JOAN

THE REBEL

"In my view the Lord and the Church are all one. It is not necessary to quibble about it. Why do you make difficulties when it is all one?" (Condemnation Trial, 17 March 1431). This is one of the most heroic and disconcerting answers that we find in the proceedings of the trial against Joan of Arc, who was put to death at the young age of nineteen (after twelve months in battle and twelve in prison). Heroic words, because they were expressed before the men of the Church, who at that time were her judges and persecutors and who, being complicit with the English, were seeking an "ideological cover" to a political trial. Disconcerting words as well, and even enigmatic, because they document the tenacious strength and acute intelligence with which the accused tried to defend herself, almost to the very end.

And yet that quibbling, that misleading use of religious language, that tribunal's ambiguity were considered by Joan's most powerful enemies to be the best way not only to kill her, but also to discredit her memory, and destroy her myth.

That is not what happened. In fact the myth, emerging even before the rehabilitation trial (1456), grew to such an extent over the centuries that whoever wishes to approach this fascinating figure of a woman must negotiate a vast sea of books, images, sermons, poetry, films, and even cartoons. Similar somewhat to the case of Francis of Assisi, it seems that many "Joans" exist, and every now and then, someone comes along who claims to have understood her fully and to be able to reveal her mystery, but instead, offers us an inaccurate and limited (or often partial) view.

In Italian historiography, the inspired volume on the "virgin warrior" written in 1998 by Franco Cardini decisively distances itself from this temptation. He reconstructs her history with rigorous adherence to sources (which are essentially the three trials: condemnation, rehabilitation, and canonization), telling this story like a novel, through a passionate affinity with the protagonist.

There is nothing to discover anew about Joan, the Maid of Orléans. If anything, we have to re-examine some aspects of her life and martyrdom.

Born in 1412 in Domrémy, a small village situated on the border of France and Lorraine, Joan was the daughter of well-to-do peasants, small landowners: her father, Jacques (whose surname only subsequently took on the form "d'Arc"), was the administrator (a sort of mayor) of the town in 1423; her mother, Isabelle, known as Romée (due to a pilgrimage to Rome?), had imparted to her daughter a Christian education expressed in ways – certainly not "primitive" – of a genuine popular religiosity. "My mother taught me the Paternoster, the Ave Maria, and the Credo. Everything I know, I learned from my mother" (Condemnation Trial, 21 February 1431), Joan reported at her trial.

The little girl grew up in a time when Christianity was being torn apart by the great Western Schism; near her village, the results were visible of that conflict (one of the numerous phases of the Hundred Years War), in which Charles, the weak heir to the throne of France, was set against the English, allies of the powerful Duke of Burgundy.

Jeannette grew up enveloped in her mother's love, playing around a tree and a spring of fresh water, with garlands of flowers, work on the loom, religious practice in the parish, and the not-too-distant echo of violence and blood: her town was faithful to the Dauphin of France, although it was surrounded by Burgundian lands, and even children clashed in skirmishes with their neighbours.

At thirteen, Jeannette suddenly had a sense of having a mission to fulfill: she had to leave for France to help "her" king. Later she would declare that the voices of the Archangel Michael and Saints Catherine of Alexandria and Margaret of Antioch had revealed this to her. Thus, within the apparent normality of an adolescent's life, perhaps slightly more serious and devoted than her contemporaries, she was in the process of preparing herself with prayer, and dedicating herself to her mission in secret. Behind her parents' backs (or at least without their consent), Joan moved, in 1428, to an uncle in Vaucouleurs, whose help she asked in acquiring permission to accompany a powerful local lord, Robert de Baudricourt. Although rejected twice, with advice to her uncle "to give her a smack," in February 1429, Robert changed his mind, and actually served as a go-between to arrange a meeting between Charles of Valois and the girl from Domrémy, eventually escorting her on a journey of around 600 kilometres, upon which Joan travelled in men's clothing, across terrain mostly under the control of the Anglo-Burgundians.

In the Castle of Chiron, in March, the meeting took place: Charles reacted uncertainly to the visit of the young woman, offering him political and military help, calling it a divine mission. The situation in and of itself was not that implausible, because there were other cases of visionary prophetesses in the area, one of whom had predicted that a "virgin girl would save the kingdom." These prophecies were even circulating around the royal court in a dramatically unfavourable moment for the twenty-seven-year-old Charles, who, from the age of seven, was a "king without a crown" and without an army capable of opposing the growing advance of the English, who, after the victory at Agincourt (25 October 1415), had conquered vast territories. Unlike in other cases, Joan, however, did not limit herself to merely talking. She wanted to fight. Moreover she wanted to reorganize and lead her army. Thus the decision for Charles was not an easy one.

After having put her to the test with the ridiculous scheme of hiding himself among his courtiers (however, Joan recognized him), the Dauphin of France listened to his unusual visitor. But he was not fully convinced. So he sent her to be judged at the University of Poitiers, which was faithful to him, while the scholars of Paris participated as the opposition. Interrogated for two weeks, Joan passed the test, got the appointment she wanted, and from then on was called the "Maid" – in other words "Virgin."

After getting some armour, an entourage, a standard, and a sword which she herself had seen in a vision (all elements that later her judges would convert into charges against her), Joan immediately set about fulfilling her mission: she inspired and led an expedition to reinforce Orléans, under siege for about six months, and managed to liberate it (8 May 1429), not without first proposing peace to the adversaries in a celebrated missive ("Letter to the English").

The military victory was not painless for the Maid, as recollected in admiring terms by the nobleman Dunois, nicknamed the "Bastard of Orléans": "She was wounded by an arrow that penetrated a half-foot into her flesh between the neck and the scapula. Notwithstanding this, she did not stop fighting and did not stop to have her wound treated."

If, during the entire war campaign, Joan's military role has never been fully clarified, and seems to be configured more in terms of her being a charismatic leader and morale booster of the army than in terms of her being an effective military commander, the siege of Orléans was an exception, because the Maid definitely decided on the strategy that overcame the English.

In the trial, Joan would testify more than once that she hadn't killed anyone in combat; moreover, she would state that, at the start of her call to service, she herself had objected to the "Voice" saying that she was only a girl, that she didn't know how to ride a horse or wage war (Condemnation Trial, 22 February 1431). It still remains a mystery, historically speaking, how a woman, not of noble birth, could have become so expert in military matters in such a short time. During the Middle Ages, not a mere few women had done battle: from the Longobard Princess Sichelgaita, who followed her husband into war and wore armour, to the more well-known Matilda of Canossa, and finally to Margaret of Tyrol. But this Maid did not grow up at court, nor could she have become sufficiently trained in such a short time: in fact, only three months had gone by from her mysterious beginnings at Vaucouleurs to the glorious triumph at Orléans!

The day after the victory, Joan immediately set out to fulfill another objective: the coronation of Charles with the Holy Chrism in the Cathedral at Reims, according to the ancient royal tradition of the Franks. The Maid of Orléans undertook the dangerous journey, escorting the Dauphin and leading his army, which defeated their enemies time and time again, until their overwhelming success at Patay (18 June) cleared the way to Reims, where the heir to the throne finally became Charles VII, king of France (17 July).

Within a few months of this event, there began the downward swing of a heroine's fortunes. Although loved by the people and the soldiers, but by few politico-military counsellors of the French court, she had become an uncomfortable thorn in the side of many: for those, for instance, who were proposing a truce

with the enemy, while Joan wished to proceed with the offen-
sive, aimed at liberating all French lands from English control.
Charles himself, who owed so much to her, seemed uncertain,
not only for reasons to do with war strategy, but perhaps because
he feared Joan's charisma, which was not easily controllable.

Everything comes to a close between August and September
of 1429. After the failure of an attempted siege in Paris and the
dissolution of the "liberation" army on the part of the king,
Joan spends the winter at court. Without the permission of the
sovereign, she resumes the military campaign in the spring of
1430, at the head of a small band of her most faithful, and on the
basis of secondary territorial directives with respect to the main
conflict. During one of these actions, in an attempt to liberate
Compiègne, Joan finds the gates of the small city closed at her
back (was it a tactical error or a betrayal?) and gets captured by
the Burgundians. It is 23 May 1430, a year after the victory at
Orléans. The king of France does not lift a finger to free her,
while the English immediately begin negotiations to acquire the
handover of their principal enemy.

Joan spends the first days of imprisonment going from one
castle to another, until she is sent to the keep of Beaurevoir castle,
where she is entrusted to the custody of three noblewomen, who
show benevolence towards her. The most influential of these,
Joan of Luxembourg, harshly admonishes her nephew (vassal to
the Duke of Burgundy), threatening to disinherit him if he ever
delivered the Maid of Orléans to the English (his aunt, however, would die at the beginning of September of the same year).
At her trial, Joan would remember the kindness of her female
wardens (who among other things bore the same name as her),
regretting having betrayed them in some way by attempting to
escape. During this attempt she fell from the tower, suffering
serious injuries. The judges would use this against her, charging
her with a presumed attempt at suicide.

The "purchase" price in the meantime was established at the conspicuous amount of 10,000 gold écus (mostly collected by means of a special tax in Normandy) and so, on 24 October 1430, Joan of Arc was sold to the English, who held her in one of their own prisons, although they entrusted judgment to an ecclesiastical tribunal, with a goal to avoid transforming her into a martyr to be feared, even after death, through an immediate and hasty execution.

From this moment on, Joan's voice, containing a surprising freshness, courage, and lucidity, rises high above the written words of the notaries, who record the interrogations taking place in Rouen, from 9 January to 30 May 1431.

It is not possible to retrace here all the phases of the trial and name each and every protagonist. They were numerous and not in the least unprepared: six Parisian university scholars, the inquisitor Jean Le Maistre, and about sixty prelates. The principal accuser was Pierre Cauchon, previous rector of the University of Paris, and in this period the bishop of Beauvais and Lisieux (where coincidentally and paradoxically Thérèse Martin was born in 1873; this woman so loved Joan of Arc, and together with her, would become the co-patroness of France).

In order to understand how an illiterate nineteen-year-old held her head up before her interrogators, it will be useful to revisit, in a more analytical way, the phases of a single hearing, such as that of 24 February 1431.

Joan points to Bishop Cauchon and urges him: "You say that you are my judge; consider well what you do; for in truth I am sent from God, and you are putting yourself in great peril." After this threatening tone, there follows a quip that is disarming in its authentic candour. She is asked if the voices revealed to her that she should escape. "I am not bound to answer you," Joan retorts without adding anything else. When she is asked then if she believes herself to be in the grace of God, her response is disarming: "If I am not, may God put me there; if I am, may He keep me there."

This is no simple shepherdess or fanatic girl! Her defence logic is lucid and intelligent, just as it had been during the Poitiers interrogations, to which Joan herself makes reference: when they point out to her that, if God had wanted to liberate France, He could have done it without intermediaries, the girl explains – touching on a theme that made the most astute theologians tremble (the relationship between Grace and freedom) – that God could have assured them of victory, but that the duty to fight rested with humans.

We hear, in a longer speech, a nostalgic re-evocation of her homeland, as well as a surrendering to emotion. When Joan is maliciously interrogated about a tree near her village, her memories pour forth: "Yes, quite close to Domremy there was a tree which was called the Ladies' tree ... Sometimes I went with other girls to make garlands to decorate the statue of Our Lady of Domrémy." Someone speaks of fairies around that tree, but Joan says she has never seen any, nor does she believe that the water from a nearby spring could cure the ill; if anything, she recalls having hung some garlands of flowers on the branches of the tree, and then she clarifies: "Ever since I learned that I must come into France, I played very little, the least that I could. And I do not know whether, since the age of reason, I danced near the tree. Sometimes I may have danced there, but perhaps I more often sang than danced." All of a sudden, the judge changes the subject and asks her: "Would you wear a woman's dress?" Joan shakes herself out of her memories, responding in a robust and provocative way: "If you give me permission, give me one, and I will take it and go. Otherwise no. I am content with this one, since it is God's will that I wear it."

In this unrelenting accusatory proceeding, only two Dominican friars were on Joan's side, advising her, as expert inquisitors, to appeal to the pope. But the English, represented in the court-room by the great uncle of Henry VI, were certainly ill-disposed to concede any kind of postponement, and the request, although legitimate, was denied.

Before the final sentence, there is a confusing scene of ab-juration, first endorsed and then retracted by Joan, whose voice seems to fade away with the passage of time. The Maid of Orléans has to be declared a heretic, a schismatic, and a devil-worshipper, her myth destroyed so as not to make of her a "political" martyr and damage that cowardly King Charles who had abandoned her to her fate.

Joan rises up like a giant among these mean and hideous schemers. When facing the distinction between the Church Tri-umphant and the Church Militant, which they unfold before her in order to force her to submit by renouncing her personal re-ligious experience, Joan resists: "I love the Church, and I wish to do everything in my power to support it in the name of our Christian faith." And then with a deep and final sigh, she utters: "I entrust myself to Our Lord, in everything."

However, on 31 May 1431, Joan of Arc is entrusted to the earthly power, which, without further ado, leads her immedi-ately to the stake. An English soldier brings her a wooden cross out of compassion, and hears her scream the name of Jesus amid the flames.

Only six years after her death, Charles of Valois triumphantly enters Paris, and around mid-century, the French re-conquer all those cities in the hands of their enemies, including Rouen. In 1455, under the authority of Pope Callixtus III, the Rehabili-tation Trial commences. In the following year all the accusations would be nullified, because the sentence of 1431 "was full of ma-licious intent, slander, iniquity, contradictions, and manifest errors, in fact as well as in law."

PART TWO

ORDINARY WOMEN

CHAPTER NINE

FLORA

AND BUSINESS

Giovanna de Cumis (known as Flora) married Pietro Grimoldi, and left Bergamo to live with her husband near the shores of the Adda River, in Trezzo, in the Milan area. From her new house, Flora could see her native city only twenty kilometres to the north: Bergamo appeared like a large whitish stain on the hills overlooking the mountains, while in Trezzo works were in full swing around the rock, looming majestically, and dropping steeply to the emerald-green waters of the river. Trezzo is a border town located at the crossroads for fugitives and the exiled, winners and losers, within the context of a struggle for power that in this period was favouring the Visconti family and their allies, the Ghibellines.

Flora, understanding full well how politics often became dangerous, predicted that a property she still owned in Bergamo could become a refuge for her husband's relatives, in case they were outlawed by the Milanese Lords. We know this from her will, drafted in 1338: we read here that the Grimoldi, being *in talli casu* (possible exile) would be able to be received *decenter* (properly) in her *habitacullum* (residence) and would pay a favourably priced rent: half the amount requested from others.

Is this favouring of her acquired relatives a sign that the marriage between Flora and Pietro was a "functioning" one? It seems so, despite the fact that the couple did not have children. On the verge of death (nine years before hers), her husband had, among other things, named her as title-holder and administrator of his assets, showing that he respected her and considered her capable from a financial point of view. Flora thus began to turn a profit out of the money received, even by lending it. A widow, however rich, has to get by.

But a similar activity awakened suspicions. For a large part of the Middle Ages, any form of loan with interest was, in fact, generally considered usury and equated with sin. The Church did not allow one to make a profit on time, since time belongs only to God. From this emerged the general condemnation of lenders, even though in practice not only Jews but many Christians conducted financial transactions, whether as private citizens or as associates of the first banking institutions. A change in the collective mentality came about by degrees from the fifteenth century on, when some religious orders realized that it was necessary to institute mutual benefit societies to support people in debt. Thus the Monte di Pietà banks (institutional not-for-profit pawnbrokers) came into being, along with similar "fair-trade" funding initiatives (to use contemporary terminology).

We have proof that in Bergamo (but not only there), such types of loans were already in effect at the beginning of the thirteenth century. In 1212, for example, a widow called Isabella entrusted a huge amount of money to the Humiliati Friars so that they could generate a profit for the benefit of her daughter. Thus a limited partnership agreement was drawn up without any suspicion.

In 1338, when she dictates her will, Flora does not, however, feel easy about the activities she had carried out. She wants to put things right, and so she clarifies her intentions in the following way: *"Vollo quo omnia male ablata per me habita … restituantur"* ("I want all the usuries committed by me to be paid back"). Consequently she organizes many offerings to the poor of Trezzo as compensation for the loans granted. She also does this, as was the custom then, with food distribution. In one bequest, for example, after having established that three units of flour be converted into baked bread, Flora makes it clear that two units of chickpeas were not to be given out in dry form, but should be seasoned or cooked in earthenware pots. Thus the poor could be assured a hot meal. I do not believe that the notary who wrote the will suggested this slight clarification. The addition was not necessary but desired: it was Flora who dictated it. And not because she was unlettered or because cooking is a female affair. These small words represent a sign of personal kindness, expressing a concern that is very feminine, and displaying traits of a mentality that knows how to connect even the lowliest particular with the Whole.

This ex-usurer then recalls her hometown, and wishes that the income acquired from her properties be distributed amongst the poorest of Bergamo. That is why she entrusts this task to the Bergamasque *Confraternita della Misericordia* (Confraternity of Mercy), which includes among its managers her relative, Yroldo de Cumis. Flora, however, wants to safeguard herself even from possible future breaches on the part of the Misericordia overseers, in the management of the property donated to them. To this effect, she establishes a provision whereby, in case the first beneficiaries were shown to be negligent in administration, the management of the inheritance would be transferred to the Friars of the Colombetta.

Like all those who experience an important turning-point in their lives, Flora demonstrates that she possesses a special determination, and, as an ex-lender of money, she knows well just how necessary it is to establish clear rules and practices, so that the monies might actually reach the legitimate heirs of her beneficence: the poor.

Besides documenting the complex theme of usury or money-lending exercised by women, the story of Flora da Trezzo is indicative of the capacity of women to operate in the financial sector. We are dealing here with a widow who has preserved her husband's patrimony and her dowry, increasing or at least maintaining the original sum. In other cases, it is even more surprising to observe this economic resourcefulness exercised by unmarried women, who operated without the constant supervision of men.

These included Bertolamina Fanoni and Beatrice Colombi, both single, and capable of administering considerable assets, at the time of the dictation of their final wishes, in 1327 and 1341 respectively.

Bertolamina Fanoni lived in the southwest area of Bergamo Bassa (Lower Bergamo). Her grandmother, Carabella, had made her will in 1253; the granddaughter made hers around seventy years later, when she was still healthy and most of all rich, indeed the architect of her enrichment, as attested in a dossier of twenty-five parchment pages, which show us three generations of a Bergamasque family in its property and emotional relationships. The Fanoni family was of rural origin (Cologno al Serio) and moved to the city in the thirteenth century. Bertolamina had a sister, Bona, and three brothers. In 1277, their father, Giovanni, had entrusted the burden of maintaining the sisters to the male members. In 1289 the two women buy a piece of land from one brother. From here on in, they are committed, in an autonomous manner, to administering and building a moderately sized estate. After having lived with a brother from 1291, the two sisters live for a short while among the Predicatori Friars (Preachers, or Dominican Friars). Then they become owners of a large house right on the Piazza di San Leonardo (today the Piazza Pontida, in the centre of Bergamo Bassa). A few years later Bona dies. In 1327, Bertolamina moves up towards the Città Alta (Upper Bergamo), near the headquarters of the Misericordia, which she nominates as beneficiary, and which thus acquires quite a bit of real estate. This woman, however, does not forget her family members, who are the recipients of the "remaining" bequests (the profits of the income from six plots of land cited in the will) together with the Predicatori Friars and the Brothers Minor (two different families belonging to the Mendicant Orders). Bertolamina also remembers a hospital, a neighbourhood confraternity, the poor of the boroughs, some women, a girl to whom she gives a dowry, her servant, and the man who works in her orchard. If Bertolamina's grandmother, in 1253, had established that thirty coins would be enough for burial expenses and for an offering to God, seventy years later her granddaughter, although unmarried, is able to dispose of many more assets, because she has prudently administered these assets and she has done it by herself.

Another single woman capable of managing her resources by herself is Beatrice Colombi, a city-dweller, although she originated from Val Cavallina, situated east of Bergamo. She may never have married, but Beatrice has a great deal to leave, when she dictates her will in 1341, and remembers the persons and places of her childhood. After naming as beneficiaries the minister of the Misericordia and her neighbourhood priest, Beatrice dictates a long list of bequests to various civic religious communities, including seven hospitals, but especially to women and the poor of the municipalities of Solto Collina, her hometown, and of Castione in the upper Seriana Valley, even remembering a certain Agnese, a hermit in the distant Scalve Valley.

Beatrice obviously maintained contact with people that lived in the mountain regions, as a surprising initiative of hers, involving a friend, demonstrates. In order to distribute salt to the poor of Solto Collina, Beatrice decides to appoint Galizia Foresti, who belonged to an eminent family of *gentiles*, or citizens living in the county. It would therefore be Galizia, with the possible collaboration of the municipality of Solto, who would monitor that what Beatrice had decided would actually get done. This appointment shows that women could also play active roles in administrative and charitable undertakings, even though the statutes of many confraternities did not provide for this (sometimes the practice outweighed the regulations!). Furthermore if we consider that Beatrice's will was drafted in the bishop's palace of Bergamo, her decision takes on greater official status and significance.

Although not belonging to the most prominent of Bergamasque aristocratic families, and although unmarried, Bertolamina and Beatrice managed their properties and were able to augment their assets through these activities.

But other women took risks in an even more dynamic sector – that of handicrafts and commerce. Let us look briefly at some examples.

Agnese Nigerzolli da Crema, also unmarried, was a linen merchant. So it is clearly stated in 1349, when she recognized that she had to return ten imperial lire (a considerable sum) for a loan that she used "*in usu merchetendie* [*sic*] *panni lini.*" Agnese did not exercise this activity by herself. After she founded a small company, at least one other woman participated in it – Leonarda, a young apprentice or associate, who would inherit all the fabrics, vases, and utensils owned by Agnese, as well as the bed and the rights of use of a workshop/room within the residence that the merchant owned, on a street on the outskirts of town.

In the same linen business sector, another woman also profitably operated – a widow called Riccadonna (meaning "rich woman") Pelabrocchi – a truly emblematic and auspicious name for a female entrepreneur! When she dictates her last will and testament in 1329, Riccadonna is living in the vicinity of San Michele al Pozzo Bianco, in the house of her brother whom she names as heir, although reserving other bequests to certain women, all relatives: her daughter, a granddaughter, her sister, and her sister-in-law. By looking at these endowments, we can reconstruct her activity as a textile merchant, because Ricca-donna names "all the linen that she owns in the village of Bol-tiere," besides quality clothing, fur coats, and a sheepskin hat.

A third example of an active Bergamasque woman in the tex-tile business (in this case wool) is documented in 1365, in the hill town of Desenzano in the Cavallina Valley: in that year, Ottabona del fu Pecino Galina, from Desenzano, commissions a certain quantity of Bergamasque wool fabric, paying in advance the amount of twenty-one lire, a truly substantial sum. This merchant of wool cloth turns out to be an unmarried woman without a father.

Certainly richer than these three women, although they were active and enterprising, would be Agnese, wife of the affluent merchant Gandino de Gandino. She lived around 1302, in the city of Bergamo. Being the wife of a merchant could be risky, and so it was for Agnese, who was kidnapped at night by two men who had a score to settle with her husband, who had died in the meantime. She was forcibly taken from Bergamo and brought to Val Seriana (the region of her birth) and, after a while, was freed by persons commissioned by the Confraternity of the Miseri-cordia Maggiore, who dealt with the ransom conditions, and in general with all of the terms necessary to settle the huge inherit-ance of the merchant. To have an idea of Agnese's wealth, it is enough to say that her husband had just given her a dress valued at ten lire (equal to around 2,000 present-day euro).

We are obviously not at the same pinnacle of wealth as that of the Venetian woman Fantina, daughter of Marco Polo, whose dowry (in around 1366) included an astonishing amount of jew-els and precious materials, but, for a provincial town like Ber-gamo, the costly dress of Agnese de Gandino is indicative of the elevated income to which a family of merchants could aspire.

The cases cited here fit into an overall panorama of women's economic dynamism, which, in the Italian region, seems to have been particularly lively in the cities on the seacoast, where the women often had to substitute for their husbands, absent on long working trips, thus acquiring much experience in the world of business.

On this same subject, there is a very suggestive case, regarding Giacoma, daughter, wife, and mother of merchants in Bari. Recognizing her skills and experience in the business sector, her son Nicola, in 1224, confers on her the authority to intervene, together with his sister and the testamentary executors, in the evaluation of administrative choices in connection with her own estate. There is also the story of the Venetian Maria, wife of the doge Pietro Ziani, who, at the beginning of the thirteenth century, participated in the financing of commercial enterprises, able, as she was, to act freely in the different sectors of economic and social life, as other of her fellow countrymen were.

In order to provide a succinct idea of the "quantity" and not only the "quality" of the work carried out by women in commercial terms, and expanding our observation to the western Mediterranean area, we only need recall the female "monopoly" in the business of head scarves and veils, exercised at the end of the fourteenth century by the women milliners of Palma di Majorca, who, on the basis of the rather favourable Catalan legislation, managed a flourishing trade between the Umbrian-Tuscan producers and Catalonia, as well as the Barbary markets.

Hence, within this lively context, Flora's lending operations, or the enterprises of the other above-mentioned Bergamasque women, were definitely not isolated cases, even if there is still much to learn about the economic entrepreneurship of medieval women within the pages of wills, expense records, and other as yet undiscovered sources.

CHAPTER TEN

AGNESINA

AND POVERTY

The plague had recently decimated the population of Bergamo, arriving late, with respect to other Italian areas, but not being more merciful in the least. And yet there were two young people intent on marrying each other, despite the fact that the environment was so inhospitable, and the couple penniless.

Her name was Agnesina, and she was fatherless, Bertolino Baroni, her father, being deceased. She had reached marriageable age, which at that time was between fourteen and sixteen. The young Agnesina worked as a servant in the home of the noble lords of Crema, who lived in the neighbourhood of San Giacomo della Porta, in the upper city. Agnesina's employers were not insensitive to the plight of the poor, because they had founded an almshouse and allowed their maids to register into the largest Bergamasque association: the Misericordia Maggiore Confraternity.

The fiancé was called Paciolo (or Pacino), perhaps hailing from Val Brembana and a resident of the city. He was definitely young; the diminutive of his name indicates that (Paciolo comes from Pace, a much-used name at the time) and so does the type of work he had done in the home of a member of the powerful

Suardi dynasty: work as a *famulus*, or *garzone* (errand-boy), boy-servant, helper in the house.

How could two penurious youths (she an orphan, he an ex-*garzone* and seemingly unemployed) establish a new family in the Bergamo of 1362?

For women, the dowry was furthermore indispensable, and requested in the marriage agreement. In our case, perhaps the betrothed themselves, or their masters, or someone else must have asked for help from the city's Confraternity of Mercy, which, for around a century, had dealt with these and similar problems. And lo and behold, twenty coins were bestowed as a dowry on Agnesina: the marriage could take place.

In this same period, 254 other girls were helped by this charitable organization in the same way. As poor as Agnesina, they belonged mostly to salaried families, or ones of artisans of modest means, who came from the country, or were immigrants on the outskirts of Bergamo. Often the girls to be married were orphans, as evidenced by the high mortality rates in the area, because of the recent plague. The fourteenth-century lists, with the names of future brides, are found in the records of offerings and expenditures that the managers of the great Misericordia Confraternity drew up with extreme care, reporting all the receipts and expenses: from the hundredweights of grain stored in the largest warehouse to the single egg distributed during an expedition into the urban neighbourhoods (the so-called *andate* or outbound missions).

Historians know how difficult it is to reconstruct the identity of the poor, to the extent that someone coined the expression "no-names" to denote the destitute. It is even more difficult to reconstruct the identity of poor women. And yet within this context, the Bergamasque Misericordia Confraternity's archive has proven to be rather generous, because it has preserved other lists with the names of its beneficiaries. The oldest of these date back to 1282, and they merit special attention, because they (along with some other lists) are unprecedented for their ingenuity and abundance, in terms of the documentation left us from the leading Bergamasque confraternity.

Those of 1282 are three rosters of names, accompanied by the certification of the quota received in clothing, distributed, in two cases, in execution of the legacies authorized respectively by Gracio de Pappis and Landolfo de Pillis, and in the third case, by autonomous decision of the Misericordia Confraternity ("*de consilio fraternitatis ... consorci Misericordiae*"). The three lists refer to the same timeframe, less than one month – between 27 November and 21 December 1282, when winter was turning bitterly cold. They were written one after the other by the same hand, that of Bergamino Marchesi, the trusted notary of the Consortium for a period of twenty years.

The first distinct list, based on twenty-one neighbourhoods, contains 208 names, the second 38, and the third 40, for a total of 286 beneficiaries. Among these, the women are in the majority, a little less than half: we count 141 of them compared to 108 adult males and 37 *pueri*, children under the age of majority. The percentage of women and children is considerably higher in the first list that posts the city's poor, divided by neighbourhood; it drops comparatively in the second and third, which also refer to the poor of the rural district, where the male beneficiaries are more numerous. This is because the number of religious volunteers in poverty increases there: Friars Minor, friars not well-identified, hermits, and recluses – all persons who had accepted the status of poverty, even if "conditional," as a consequence of a religious choice.

Among the 141 female beneficiaries, the unmarried outnumber the married. Just within the first list we count 84 single women, 15 married, and 13 widows. Unlike for the wealthy classes, where there could be cases of independent, rich, and enterprising single women (as we have seen in the previous chapter), for the poor girls, not marrying aggravated their situation, and constituted great financial insecurity, either as a cause (the absence of a dowry) or as an effect (a wretched single state, or a permanent precariousness). They thus had to provide, all by themselves, for their own subsistence. The first Bergamasque Misercordia list indicates how it could happen, highlighting two additional subgroups in the category of single laywomen: 10 girls live within their own family or in the custody of another, while 39 are in service to another, like the young Agnesina with whom we began.

Being a household helper and domestic worker represented a source of subsistence for many girls and women, who however continued to remain below the recognized threshold of poverty, while other female servants, in the same period, managed to stay above that same threshold, and appear, for example, among those registered in the Misericordia Confraternity, or among those who offered, and did not necessarily receive, assistance. This perhaps depended on the different salary level, age, and relationship with employers.

And now let us look at the Saint's Day of these servant girls (though for 14 of them, the name is not given), because it is lovely to find, even if in a fragmentary manner, the appearance of people who have been left for so long in absolute obscurity (I present here the names in the order as found in the first list): Richelda (2), Gisla (2), Carina, Bella, Pasqua, Guglielma, Dorata, Bonafemmina, Riccadonna (meaning "rich woman" and thus a mockery of a name for a poor person!), Agnese, Mazarasse, Martina, Pasina, Ymelda, Sibilla, Benvenuta, Bresciana (2), Margherita. No "surname" appears in the group, except for that of Pasina de Pella. On the other hand, some nicknames are suggestive, such as Tetaegia (Old Tit), a teasing name for an aged and poor spinster.

Besides the servants, among those poor women, assisted by the Misericordia Confraternity, in 1282, there is mention of some sick women: two blind women ("Ottabella *que dicitur* Croppa *que non videt* [who could not see]; Gisla Fachi de Triscurio *que non videt*"); a paralytic ("*filia* Rubei de Caleppio *que est asidrata*," "daughter of Rubei de Caleppio who was paralytic"); and a deaf woman ("*surda de Mediolano*," "the deaf woman of Milan").

Illness or age could definitely constitute a cause of poverty, even for people falling from a once well-to-do status. In the Middle Ages these cases were called the "disgraced poor." Some of the women cited in the Misericordia Confraternity lists seem to belong to this category. It is important to note in particular the fall from grace of the de Cumis lineage, which was known to be wealthy and cultured. On the one hand, an old woman appears on the first list – the mother of the master, the "*magister* Iohannes de Cumis*," and on the other, a boy, the father still alive, "*unus ex pueris Guillelmi de Cumis*." Childhood and old age, the vulnerable ages – these are the first victims of impoverishment.

On the lists of 1282, the case of religious women considered poor is much more complex.

There are the women hermits who live alone, outside the city, and in the forest. Within this group there are "Pomma *que stat super montem Sancti Iohannis*" ("Pomma who lives on Mount Saint John") and "Malgarita *que stat super montem de Rasollo*" ("Malgarita living on top of Mount Rasollo"). There are also the recluses, who lived that extreme form of penitence, widespread at the time, consistent with voluntary incarceration; and, in fact, on the lists, these are regularly called "*incarzelate*" ("incarcerated"), a term assuming a precise and unambiguous meaning. There are eight women: "*incarzelata que stat in domo Sancte Catarine*"; "Donagisla [or lady Gisla] Çini *incarzelata*"; "Anexia de Albano *incarzelata*"; "Cossina Soyari *incarzelata*"; "*incarzelata* de Bonate*"; "*incarzelata* de Albano*"; "*incarzelata vicinie Sancti Stephani*"; "Pomma de Zonio *incarzelata que stat in stricta de Lissono*"; to whom may be added "Flora-mons *que stat prope pontem de Piniolo*" ("Floramons who lives near the Piniolo Bridge"), the bridges being a place of choice for the voluntary recluses. But I have the impression that other recluses are hidden behind names that do not explicitly reveal their situation. Some of the "poor women" are in religious institutions or hospitals, and it is not known whether they are there as patients, servants, or *incarzelate*: Benda and Margherita are living "*ad domum Sancti Martini*"; the recluse Cossina Soyari lives in the rural hospital of Almenno, just as the *incarzelata* of Albano lives at the urban hospital of Santa Caterina. The attestation of Arnolda "*que stat in domo Umiliatorum de Vaçine*" is important for the history of the local Humiliati. Two women who make us think, directly or indirectly, about eccentric and well-known religious experiences are "Richafina *que dicitur Apostolla*" ("named the Apostle") and "*una uxor quondam illius de Profeta*" ("a widow, whose husband was called the Prophet").

It is also very apparent that, in this early period, the Confraternity beneficiaries – whether male or female – were, generally speaking, not beggars without a fixed address, but the poor that lived in their own or someone else's house. We notice for this reason a very specific strategy, on the part of the Bergamasque Misericordia, towards them, in comparison to the seemingly similar confraternity experiences elsewhere: there was no establishment of shelters, nor special refuges that singled out the marginal; but there was a total presence within the social fabric, however unwholesome, an out-and-out pursuit, and ultimately a discovery and recognition of situations of distress – in other words, a strategy of integration and not of exclusion, of proximity and not of distance. This was achieved through a network of information that reached the confraternity directors through the registered members themselves, neighbourhood by neighbourhood. Once information was received, provisions were made to collect food, money, or clothing to distribute through a dense web of volunteers; suffice it to say that there were 44 (two per neighbourhood) of them involved in the above-mentioned expedition of 1282, when articles of clothing were brought to 208 poor folk.

In the first century of its history, precisely because of the effectiveness of its assistance to the poor, Bergamo's Misericordia Confraternity attained the trust of hundreds of men and women that supported it with donations and collaboration. It would be interesting to learn what the judgment was of those who received help from the Misericordia, and, in particular, of the destitute women beneficiaries. Some episodes may be able to shed some light on this uncertainty, allowing us to observe these women from a closer vantage point.

The first is paradoxical because it involves a group of "penitent thieves." In the spring of 1296, violent civil war broke out in Bergamo: a member of the Colleoni family had killed Giacomo Mozzi of the *consorteria* (association of noble wealthy medieval families with mutual interests) of the powerful Suardi family, who set fire to the headquarters of the episcopacy and the *podestà* (municipal authority). Taking advantage of the unrest, many succeeded in entering the Misericordia granary and emptied it, carrying away 94 loads and 4 *sextarii* (a liquid and dry measurement) of wheat. It was more than a metric ton, a substantial quantity. The theft hit the confraternity hard. It is common knowledge that plundering for reasons of hunger was commonplace in time of war, and the well-stocked warehouse of the Misericordia whetted the appetite of many. Among them were even some women, three of whom touch upon our story, because they are cited among those who, surprisingly, returned a few days later to give back to the confraternity what they had wrongfully taken. About thirty or so persons restored, in all, 8 loads and 5 sextarii, about 7–8 quintals (a quintal = 100 kg) of wheat.

Some are really down and out: they include, among others, two carriers of wine kegs strapped to their shoulders, a servant, and an orphan boy, who all by himself returns a *sextarius*, or 16 kg, of wheat. In the group there are three repentant women: dona Duncia Martini Bordiga, dona Delgada, servant of the Crema family, and an anonymous woman ("*quaedam mulier*") living at the suburban almshouse of Saint Anthony. In terms of these last two, we can assume, with considerable certainty, that they lived in extreme poverty, and therefore their gesture acquires an even greater significance.

Of course, those thieves that did not repent, and did not return the spoils, were many more – if we make the calculations, about two to three hundred must have participated in the looting of the granary! But these thirty alone, ones who really needed that flour, perhaps more than the others, are enough to give us a sense of what the Misericordia Confraternity meant to the Bergamasque community. They felt they could not eat the bread of the Misericordia, bread destined to feed the poor, just like them.

Another episode that allows us to witness the world of the poverty of women reveals the identity of a woman from the countryside. In 1363, she requests help for her sick son, and, indirectly, confirms the sense of trust which people even in those areas far from the city felt for the Misericordia Confraternity of Bergamo.

In Comun Nuovo, a hamlet on the plain about ten kilometres from Bergamo, there lived a woman called Belinsenia, the widow of a man called Pendolo. One of her sons suffered from the "sickness of stones" or calculosis (we are not sure if they were kidney stones, urinary tract stones, liver stones, or gallstones). The "sickness of stones" is the ancient generic expression: it is spoken of in the Hippocratic Oath and it indicates a pathology that could only be cured by means of surgery. At the end of the thirteenth century we know that, in Bergamo, to have a doctor make a house call cost a great deal of money, especially if the illness required prolonged care. In such a case, it was necessary to draw up a contract through a notary. This happened in 1283 with Giovanni de Pillis, suffering from an infection (an abscess) to a lower limb. He had a rich father who paid the doctor, a certain Master Uberto da Bonate, a steep fee (4 lire, equivalent to about 800 euro) for his house visits, which he would have had to conduct until the son was cured.

But how could someone like Belinsenia, a poor widow with children, living in the countryside, afford the luxury of such care?

Enter the Misericordia Confraternity, who helped this anonymous child, just like all the other needy sick children whose parents could not afford to pay for medical care. The person who undertook this care was Magister Donato da Almenno, who was no hack to be sure: in fact he had acted for the Confraternity on other occasions; but it is not clear if, in this case, he assisted a child already operated on by others ("*pro uno suo filio inciso*": the scribe for the Misericordia was kindly in his use of the word "*inciso*" meaning "cut into" whereas others would have used the word "*secatus*" meaning "slice into"), or whether he himself had executed the surgery. The fee of 20 coins (around 20 euro), in the absence of any comparison, seems appropriate, whatever his task.

We do not know the outcome of the operation on that poor country urchin, but we do know that the request for assistance from his mother to the Confraternity of Mercy was heeded to a degree that we may define as highly specialized for that era.

Besides the truly poor, then as now, there were those who pretended to be so, in order to receive support. One of these was Bettina de Antea, who in 1380 asked the municipal government to force the Misericordia directors to pay her a pension for life. The woman states that she and her husband were at risk of becoming poverty-stricken, because her father Lorenzo had ended up in prison for debts, while the Confraternity had inherited from her uncle, Giovanni de Antea, a huge endowment. The Confraternity managers rejected the request, replying accurately and precisely: Bettina was not poor, because she was in possession of several homes in Bergamo and of country properties. She had just sold a property to an associate of the Confraternity, and besides, Lorenzo de Antea was not in jail but freely walking the streets of Bergamo. A fake pauper who asked for assistance: this seems to be the story of Bettina de Antea, but the Misericordia does not let itself be deceived, and makes it quite clear that it has to give priority to the women and girls who are truly impoverished: women about to give birth, the sick, widows, the elderly, or single women wishing to marry.

And the needs continue to grow because the poverty situation worsens in the late fourteenth century, in Bergamo and in other places, where new legal provisions limit the flow and circulation of beggars. In the Late Middle Ages the poverty-stricken undergo a change. The kind of poverty that I would define as "domestic" is now flanked by that of the homeless, and for them it is well-nigh impossible to reconstruct an identity.

The method of providing assistance on the part of the Misericordia also changes. The Confraternity abandons that peculiar custom of outings into the neighbourhoods (and beyond) in order to reach the needy. From the middle of the fourteenth century this practice was substituted by the use of the "bonus," a kind of licence that was given to the poor and which they had to present at the Confraternity headquarters to receive food or charity – a little like ration books during the Second World War. Thus the poor had to have a "ticket" to take to the Misericordia and access the charity to be handed out.

Perhaps this change was necessary for security reasons, given the continuous worsening of the political and military situation, and an already endemic state of civil war; another reason could have been the need to have stricter control over distribution and the identity of the recipients. But the chief reason must have been a question of logistics: the mechanism of the outings into the community, with the direct distribution of food and charity, had become too complicated and onerous. It was much easier to use the licence system. It would still be necessary to recruit volunteers to complete the tasks, but in a much smaller quantity, compared to the previous community outings. From the point of view of the poor on the receiving end, the new system had the advantage of increasing the opportunities to access the benefits: in 1363 this is what happened, for instance, three times per week, except in special circumstances when temporarily the rhythm of distribution decreased. Previously, the benefits were apportioned out only every fifteen days, and alternating Sundays. This was ultimately a functional rationalization: time and human resources were being saved. Something was lost, because the previous regime truly displayed the experience of the Misericordia, through the streets of Bergamo and the outskirts, in a visible way. But the original and specific mission of the Confraternity was maintained – a real and personal interchange between benefactors and beneficiaries, as well as a gleaning of direct knowledge of the conditions of social malaise, a malaise well-displayed in the images of beggars painted in the margins of many fifteenth-century frescoes portraying the lives of the saints.

Along with the modern era begins a different chapter in the history of impoverished men and women, unfortunately one into which I cannot venture.

In terms of the thirteenth and fourteenth centuries, I end my account at the names and small stories of the people I have presented, such as that of Agnesina, who wished to marry; of Belinsenia, who feared for the life of her sick son; of an anonymous repentant thief, who returned the stolen grain; and of Bettina, who did not repent of having tried to deceive, and who was not poor in the least.

CHAPTER ELEVEN

OTTEBONA

AND MARRIAGE

As a good union must be between a husband and a wife, who in the time
of their youth and in the time of their old age, have loved, and continue to
love, and will wish to love each other, before His divine Majesty.

These words are not recorded in a canonical treatise on marriage, nor a literary work, nor even in a moral or theological sermon on conjugal love. They are actually found in the fold of a long parchment document, dated 1309, written by a notary under dictation by a woman called Ottebona Uliveni, who was intent on settling her last will and testament while she still enjoyed good health, with all her mental and physical faculties intact, despite no longer being young nor having the benefit of peace of mind, given that she was alone and separated from the man she loved.

A wife and relative of notaries, Ottebona was in no way feeble-minded. She knew what she was doing and she weighed her words carefully, as her will demonstrates. It was drafted with lucidity and mindfulness in a particularly difficult moment for her. Her husband, Pietro Lorenzoni da Vertova, was, in fact, very far away. He was forced to stay on the other side of the Adda River, in Milanese territory, because the city of Bergamo had exiled him for reasons that our sources do not make clear, but could have something to do with outstanding debts, or with the ongoing clashes at the time between the Guelphs (mostly escaped into the valleys) and the Ghibellines (still residing in the city).

Hence in 1309, within the harsh context of violence, and after at least thirty years of marriage, Ottebona and Pietro are forced to separate, although they remain united by affection and common interest, such that Ottebona makes her will as if her husband is present and consenting, "*tamquam et si dictus Petrus esset presens in propria persona*"; and she feels the need to dictate a clause in order to share before God ("*coram Deo omnipotenti et coram eius mayestate*") the spiritual fruits they have harvested together, using words that go beyond legal language – those words that I cited in my opening and that now I present in Latin: "*Tamquam et sicut bona societas viri et uxoris qui et que ad invicem condam tempore iuventutis et senectutis eorum diligerunt et diligent et cupient se diligere coram predicta Mayestate.*"

Thus Ottebona expresses herself, stipulating that all the charity and prayers offered up in the past or in the near future, by husband or wife or both together, be presented to God in mutual agreement. In that time this was considered a great gift, the ultimate gift that one could give to one's beloved (even if today such a sentiment is perhaps difficult to understand).

The Latin verb "*diligere*" (meaning "to esteem, to love") appears three times in the text. It is an explicit word in affective terms, but certainly not a necessary one to conclude an economic-legal agreement which substantially amounts to a will. "*Diligere*" reveals a feeling and a judgment intentionally expressed by this woman, who recalls, in an important moment in her life, what has characterized the essential value of her marriage, defined, among other things, most effectively and "practically" as a union or partnership (*societas*).

So Ottebona and Pietro loved each other. Love had been for them a living reality at the heart of their marriage: a fact that is by no means a foregone conclusion, then, just as today, but not impossible, then, just as today.

The two were not nobles; they belonged to two upper-middle-class families, the Uliveni and the Lorenzoni families, both of notarial origins, coming from the mountain region, and then drifting toward the city. In Vertova, in the Seriana Valley, the Uliveni family traded in wool, and held positions in the local municipal government. Pietro Lorenzoni, in the seventh decade of the thirteenth century, still worked as a notary in his hometown; from 1290 on, he seems to have been living in Bergamo, in the neighbourhood of Sant'Andrea, where he practised his notarial profession, together with a lending business. In this urban environment, a relative of Ottebona practised the notarial profession: that Giovanni Uliveni who, in the first forty-year period of the fourteenth century, was a very important figure in the city. Twenty times he exercised the role of general minister of the Misericordia Maggiore, the largest Bergamasque Confraternity, and in this role he also attempted to end the fierce factional battles. He was the last minister who gave space to women (approximately two thousand) participating in the large reality of this charity organization, an institution that already in the fourteenth century acted like a sort of "parallel municipality" to the official one. He supported moreover some nunneries, such as that of the Poor Clares, and the association responsible for restorations and financial aid to the Church of Santa Maria, a major church in upper Bergamo. And finally he controlled the management of huge sums of money, never enriching himself, evidenced by his will, which attests to only moderate assets.

We are also aware of a daughter of Ottebona and Pietro – Detesalva, who, thirty years after her mother, in 1336, would dictate her will, demonstrating in turn affection towards her own husband, Gerardo Tiraboschi, already mentioned by his mother-in-law in 1309, and having died in the meantime. In

Ordinary Women

her last will and testament, Ottebona's daughter does not use the verb "*diligere*," but she does perform an equally significant act in memory of her spouse: after his death, Detesalva wishes to be buried next to Gerardo and stipulates that frescoes be painted on the sepulchral monument of her husband. Similar wishes are to be found in other wills by wives, and not just Bergamasque ones.

Ottebona and Detesalva, mother and daughter, do not belong to the aristocracy. Although their lives are characterized by a certain amount of affluence, they do come close to the lives of ordinary folk. And it is among the stories of these commoners, and from sources often considered of minor importance, that new perspectives may emerge on the emotional and love bonds that were present in medieval marriages.

It is in fact appropriate to raise once again a question already posed by several historians. Chronicles and romances speak of marriages of nobles and knights. This type of union is often dominated by preoccupations with social prestige. At the front and centre of the nuptial contract lie the family strategies and designs. But what do we know about the marriages contracted between commoners? And by commoners, I do not only mean the peasants and salaried citizens (who could marry more freely, not having much or anything at all to share), but also those persons belonging to the middle and upper-middle classes.

Research conducted in the last decades, specifically dealing with notarial documentation, has, in part, answered this question, and what has come to light is often more positive than we might have imagined, as evidenced by Ottebona's little story. Love could flourish even in a medieval marriage.

Studies have also confirmed another tendency that characterizes the evolution of family structures in the Late Middle Ages: the reducing of the "extended" family to the marital couple, as the great Italian historian Cinzio Violante revealed so many years ago. His observations, corroborated, on the basis of notarial documents, by other scholars (David Herlihy, for one), are in line with those of an expert on feudal marriages in France, Georges Duby, according to whom, from the twelfth century on, lineage seems to have given way to the conjugal unit, the couple.

And in this couple, what margins of freedom in her movements were available to the female side of the dyad? Were women acting autonomously, or were their wishes conditioned by influences, or even pressures, from others? These questions are unavoidable and, in fact, recurring in the discussions of historians.

In the first place, it is necessary to ask what assets were conceded to women, and in particular, to married women. We are speaking of the Bergamasque situation, which was similar to, but also different from, others; many were the local variants around the legal capacity for a woman's asset ownership. Unfortunately we cannot linger on this issue. In all cases, the norms regulating the matter were established by laws and by customs – in other words, by the municipal statutes. For instance, they agreed to appoint certain personages to safeguard the legal actions of women. In Bergamo these were the *mundoald* (the guardian) and the guarantor-judge.

Bergamo followed Longobard traditions, and therefore the institution in effect was that of the *mundium* (the law of protection), which entrusted the control and legal protection of the woman to the mundoald. This could not be the husband, but was another close relative (father, brother, son, cousin). In the absence of sons, the mundoald was the legitimate heir. After the disappearance of the institution of the mundoald, which happened in the years between the end of the thirteenth century and the first decades of the next, in the various deeds executed by single women or widows, there is no male figure mentioned who plays the role of giving consent or of protection: thus these women act on their own (obviously with the help of a notary and witnesses). On the other hand, the consent of the husband is necessary for married women: a legacy of Roman law, now in the form of common law.

Once the figure of the mundoald no longer plays a role, the requirement of the husband's consent comes into play; but soon after, the requisite for a guarantee of a woman's freedom from someone outside of the family was put into effect – in the person of the guarantor-judge, introduced in Bergamo by the statute of 1331.

Although we cannot speak in a real sense of "autonomy," "absence of freedom" is not something we observe, because the woman *is* playing a role, just as is demonstrated by the financial activities carried out by these women making their wills. The guarantor-judge seems to perform a function to protect this freedom, rather than to limit autonomy.

The actual implementation of these legal procedures can be verified through notarial sources: endowment allocations, engagement contracts, and especially wills. If a woman made a will it was because she had her own assets to liberally dispose of (within certain limits): she did not want to leave them to the normal mechanisms of legitimate succession. It is necessary to distinguish between the two different marital states: single women could dispose of assets inherited; married women, of assets originating from marriage.

Let us linger on these last elements. When the marriage was contracted, the woman had her paternal dowry at her disposal and, generally speaking, the two gifts from her husband: the first was called the *meta* or the *quarta* (depending on the size of the corresponding marital estate), while the second was the wedding gift, the *donatio propter nuptias*, said in the Roman way, or the *morgengabe*, the morning gift, said (more beautifully) in the Longobard way. More precisely, the *meta/quarta* gift was to be bestowed at the time of the engagement, the *morgengabe* after the wedding night. These are the assets, augmented or reduced through time, of which the woman could dispose in her will, with her husband alive. Vice versa, the husbands' wills are also significant, where they dictate specific arrangements to the benefit of – or often to the detriment of – the living wife.

But the most frequent case is that of the widowed testatrix (female testator), because a married woman more often made her will after the death of her husband.

In Bergamo, the widowed testatrices are often women who pass on their dowry or inheritance from their family of origin, or women who demonstrate that they have administered the assets received through the husbands' marital gifts. The husband could in fact pass on (with or without restrictive clauses) a part of his assets to his wife, who is nominated either as the usufructuary or even as the proprietor. If however she is named as the guardian of minor children, her administrative authority is generally limited, only lasting until the attainment of the heirs' age of majority.

Let us now look more closely at specific examples. The whole process of the legacy of the Bergamasque Cardinal Guglielmo Longhi, a friend of Petrarch, is most complicated, and it is a story in which many women, and especially a widow, play protagonist roles. The cardinal had named his grandson Giacomo Longhi as heir to his vast fortune. This heir was married to Bona Carpioni, and had had three daughters, Franceschina, Viridina, and Gisla, married to representatives of prestigious local families. Giacomo died in 1319; Bona gave birth to a son after this death, and being the only male, he inherited his father's wealth. Here we have the typical case of a widow, mother, and guardian of a small son, who administers the boy's assets long-term. Between 1319 and 1321 she draws up an inventory of these. In order to ostensibly invest a part of the enormous sums of inherited money, Lady Bona makes a series of land purchases in villages adjacent to Bergamo. But Giacomino dies as a child, in 1325. So the mother transfers the legacy to her three daughters, two of whom are aided by their husbands, while Franceschina, already a widow, is represented by an attorney. After a period of about twenty years, Bona, remarried in the meantime, and once again a widow without having had more sons, makes her will: she is still in possession of significant assets, and she leaves them to the two surviving daughters, in an effort to put an end to the ongoing fights between one and the other and the heirs of the third.

We can also find a prolonged management by women of substantial property, in less eminent social environments. The above-mentioned Flora da Trezzo, in the absence of sons, is for a decade the title holder of her deceased spouse's assets, in the capacity of *"domina et massaria et ussufructuaria et rogataria et fidecomissaria bonorum rellictorum suprascripti condam domini Petri mariti"* ("proprietress, administrator, usufructuary, beneficiary of legacies, and charged with the distribution of the offerings established by her deceased husband Pietro"). The case of Urielda Punioni is also interesting. She charges her daughter Alberta, already established as her heir, to administer, as trustee, all her charitable bequests destined to the poor.

Up till now we have predominantly considered economic issues, but marriage represents, for the medieval mentality, something more than a simple contract; nor is it only an institution, but rather a sacrament, namely "an effective sign of Grace." It is interesting to note, in this respect, that the margins of economic-legal autonomy for the married woman were established after canonical law and theology made significant steps in matrimonial matters. This happened starting in the twelfth century.

Within the theological sphere, in particular, the deliberations surrounding the Mother of God influenced the collective mentality, through the diffusion of images, prayers, and chants that revealed the human feeling of Mary, who experienced joy and pain in embracing, nursing, watching over, and then seeing her son grow and die. More and more, Mary appeared like the "new Eve" who redeemed the role of woman, and as the Mother who had shared the fate of so many other mothers.

Thus it can be asked: is it possible to establish a link between the development of the devotion to Mary, and real progress in the female condition in the medieval West? I believe so. But such an unambiguous yes on this point comes from historians much more distinguished than me, and ones representing different ideological positions. For example, Jean Leclercq, a true expert in medieval monastic literature and curator of the complete works of Bernard of Clairvaux, was convinced of this. And so was the layperson Jacques Le Goff, who has in fact stated:

> If one thinks that the cult of the Virgin Mary happened
> simultaneously with the transformation in the marriage
> sacrament, in the promotion of childhood and the nu-
> clear family, as demonstrated by the images of the nativity
> in this period, one should see in the Virgin the great ally
> of the earthly destiny of woman.

This great French medievalist was also convinced that theological thought around Mary benefited from the development of courtly love: "Our Lady is the 'lady' of the knight in her most elevated form, the 'lady' of men, the irradiance of a female figure in the divine and the human world of medieval society."

Medieval canonistic and theological literature is obviously more austere than chivalric romances, and yet it exercised, in fact, a major influence on daily life, by declaring that the free choice of spouses and mutual affection were the foundations of marriage, of its legitimacy and validity. Although the principle was established, it didn't of course mean that practice conformed in every case to theory, but at least law and theology certified that marriage should be built on free consent. And this was not inconsequential.

One theological current of thought even exalted conjugal love as a form of mutual affection, physical as well, freeing it from those suspicions that the moralistic ideas of the time had raised about sexuality. The "hard liners" based themselves mainly on texts from Saint Jerome and exacerbated forms of asceticism. The others cited the Song of Songs and all those evangelical episodes in which Jesus spoke very well of women, love, and marriage (dating from the feast of Cana!).

In the twelfth century, praise for conjugal love was in vogue among many monastic authors: from Saint Bernard, who situated marital affection on a love scale leading towards union with God; to Peter the Venerable, who cherished the marital experience of his parents, and who consoled Heloise, promising her that, after the death of Abelard, she would in future re-embrace her beloved in Heaven; to the Abbess of Bingen, the great Hildegard, who, as we have seen, used passionate wording to refer to the physical union between a husband and wife.

Therefore, there did not exist in the Middle Ages only two extreme positions, the contempt for sexuality and the exaltation of free love, the first represented by the "erotophobic" clerics and the other by the "hedonistic" carefree spirits. There was also the life of ordinary people: those who loved their wife or husband, or who had learned to love them along the way, perhaps regardless of how the marriage began. These people did not have the time to read chivalric romances, in which love was idealized, nurtured by a sentimental impetus or an aesthetic instinct as in an ideal and courtly dream.

I have asked myself many times, in fact: is it possible that marital love was born in the twentieth century, when (thanks to sacrosanct struggles) the choice of a partner became free in the truest sense from parental control? And before? Did it just not exist? Have we been procreating down through the centuries inside a "family" institution akin to a kind of cage that has shut out our feelings?

Without doubt, much pain was endured within the domestic walls of many unions. And on this subject, we can recount stories and even collect songs, such as those of the unhappily married, a genre that boasts a well-recognized tradition. But there also exist other songs and love letters between spouses, as suggested by the story of Ottebona, of her daughter, and of many other wives in love, whose voices have reached us, after seven centuries, via sources decidedly unpretentious and modest, but unequivocal in their delicate sincerity.

CHAPTER TWELVE

GRAZIA

AND THE RELIGIOUS LIFE

In the heart of the thirteenth century, Grazia d'Arzago was the abbess of Santa Grata, the oldest and most famous Bergamasque nunnery, founded, according to tradition, by the woman who had collected the remains of the body of Alexander the martyr, and who had fostered the introduction of Christianity into the city at the beginning of the fourth century.

The abbess of Santa Grata was an important person in Bergamo: the bishop even rendered public homage to her every year, stopping during a procession at the door of the nunnery and offering a palm branch.

Grazia belonged to the noble family of the harbour masters of the region of the Gera d'Adda, episcopal vassals of Cremona in the eleventh century and, already in the twelfth, linked as well to the bishop of Bergamo. Arzago today is still a small town on the plain, as green and irrigated as the fields are, as one descends towards the lower Bergamasque plain. Grazia climbed from these lands toward the city around 1227, at which time she was already a part of the monastic community, which received only members of the highest aristocracy.

Though she was an important figure, knowledge about Grazia d'Arzago dates from the fairly recent historiographic era, while this abbess, without doubt, deserves greater consideration, having been one of the most distinguished, cultured, and determined women of medieval Bergamo. Aware of the hyperbole, I would like to identify her as a sort of local Hildegard von Bingen, a lover of culture and open to the world outside the cloister.

Grazia d'Arzago led the nunnery for more than a forty-year period, from 1229 to the middle of the seventh decade of the thirteenth century. It is a long period characterized by strong governmental action: the abbess and her delegates even left the seclusion of the convent (not so strict before the fourteenth century) in order to inspect the monastic properties, grouped mostly in towns close to the city (Albegno, Calvenzano, Grassobbio, and Stezzano). The nuns also prudently extricated themselves from the plotting of some dishonest administrators, such as Lanfranco da Chignolo, who pocketed 14 imperial lire from the sale of monastic lands. Grazia even obtained a pontifical privilege in 1235 and reiterated before Bishop Giovanni Tornielli, against the claims of Pope Gregory IX, that her community did not intend to follow the Cistercian model, which was very strict in terms of the female cloistered life.

Grazia d'Arzago had in mind another type of reform, and talked about it with a man of eminent cultural standing: Pinamonte da Brembate, the Dominican friar, who in 1265 wrote the Rule of the Confraternity of the Misericordia Maggiore and who charismatically led the Confraternity in its first years. The abbess entrusted him with the task of reconstructing the biography of Santa Grata. Just as Pinamonte was spreading the ideal of the Misericordia Confraternity among laypersons, men and women, so did Grazia intend to present anew the cult of the founding saint.

The abbess, in fact, wished to promote a programme of re-ligious renewal which would return to the original ideals and which would be depicted through a cycle of images in illumin-ated manuscript form on the *Vita Sanctae Gratae* (the Life of Saint Grata) or frescoed on the walls of the nunnery. Standing out from among these highly valuable iconographic documents of great quality are the miniature of the Dominican friar who offers the book he has written to the nuns (portrayed in light-coloured garments) and a fresco representing Grazia herself as she kneels and offers the same manuscript to the founder of the nunnery.

One of the central episodes of the life of Santa Grata was the practice of charity, through, among other things, the foundation of a hospice. Charity and culture represent a two-pronged vo-cation that binds Pinamonte da Brembate and Grazia d'Arzago. The former had contributed to the founding of a fraternity that dedicated itself to providing assistance; the latter was taking up once more, as her central theme, the ideal of charity that had been promoted by the founder of her religious community. So at this point, we are less surprised to discover that our abbess de-cided to enrol herself along with her nuns into the lay Confra-ternity of the Misericordia, together with about fifty laywomen residing in the neighbourhood around the convent, in the heart of the Upper City. The example of Grazia d'Arzago was followed by the Benedictine nuns of Valmarina, a small town just north of the city hills, and by the nuns of Bonate Sotto, a rural town west of Bergamo, on the so-called Island between the Brembo and the Adda Rivers.

The affiliation of nuns (belonging to two urban convents and one rural one) to the Misericordia Confraternity is inter-esting, given that monastic affiliations with lay confraternities were not very common. In the cenobitic setting, the confrater-nal experience is, in fact, mostly linked to a spiritual fraternity or to a group of laypersons associated with a monastery, while the nuns recorded in the Bergamasque register belong to an external confraternity, and are inscribed at the same level as the other laywomen.

Grazia d'Arzago's choice confirms that it was possible to communicate beyond the walls of the female monasteries, in a much livelier exchange of ideas and relationships than one might imagine. She recognized that something could be learned even from laypeople, showing that she did not conceive of monasticism as an "enclosed garden."

Grazia had therefore "crossed over the wall," while continuing to live within the cloister.

Other religious women chose to live a solitary and somewhat risky life, completely without any walled-in or human protection – I am referring to the hermits.

One of these was Sister Bergamina, *remitta de Hendine*, the (female) hermit of Endine. She, too, registered with the Misericordia Confraternity of Bergamo at the same time as Grazia d'Arzago, around 1270.

The village of Endine faces the small lake of the same name, almost halfway through the Cavallina Valley, along the old road that still leads from Bergamo towards the northeast, to Lovere and further north into the Camonica Valley. Together with merchants, soldiers, and travellers, what also journeyed along this route were ideas and ideals. Indeed, the Cavallina Valley hosted within its territory monastic establishments, houses of the Humiliati Friars, and hermitages. In 1282 we know of five *remitti vallis Cavaline* (Cavallina Valley [male] hermits) who were receiving wool clothing from the Misericordia Confraternity, while our hermit Bergamina appears on the Confraternity's female Register. We also know that in the distant Scalve Valley there lived another woman hermit. Unfortunately we do not have, at least not yet, evidence of similar experiences among women in the other Bergamasque valleys, since they are closed off to the north by the mountains, and therefore much more difficult to traverse for wayfarers and pilgrims.

The hermit's life represents the solitary existence *par excellence*. How then could the hermit of Endine come to know about the city's Misericordia Confraternity well enough to become a member?

It is probable that Bergamina's hermitage may not have been situated along the steep and forested slopes of the valley, but close to the road that runs along the lake. Often women hermits lived, in fact, near bridges or along transport routes; this also facilitated their solicitations of alms. Furthermore, people in search of advice frequently sought out hermits, and Bergamina could have learned, during these dialogues, about this city initiative, stemming from the Misericordia Confraternity.

There lie between these two extreme poles – the cultured abbess, living in the heart of the city, and the solitary hermit living in the valley – many other experiences that document the existence of a lively and diversified female religious movement that flourished in Bergamo as it did elsewhere.

The most conspicuous traces are visible in the twelfth century and involve again the rural areas, usually more difficult to find out about compared to the city.

Among the female communities in the countryside, a particularly interesting story is that of San Pietro near Urgnano, where, at the beginning of the twelfth century, a woman of means from this place, by name of Berlenda, founded a small monastery and, with the help of two other women and of a lay brother, cultivated the fields with her own hands. The three women came up against some very hard work, since the earth was full of stones and unturned soil, as it happens to be in all the zones of the Bergamasque central plain, close to the Serio River. This endeavour, initiated by Berlenda, would not last long and died out over the course of a century, but its value remains as proof of the strength which a woman could call upon in her effort to realize the original Benedictine ideal, even though she lived on the periphery of the great centres of reformed monasticism.

Concurrent to Berlenda's endeavour was the appearance in Redona, at the gates of Bergamo, of a double religious community, in which the women had authority over the men. The Augustinians of San Giorgio in Redona established a small religious house that re-introduced, in such a peripheral area as the Bergamasque province, a model analogous to that of Fontevrault and other more famous experiments, in which a unique prominence was afforded to women. Yet again in the year 1309, after more than a century and a half since the origin, Bergamo's bishop officially reaffirmed the prerogative of the women governing over the men, who, instead, laid claim to the possibility of exercising greater power, including administrative power. The bishop, using the statutes of foundation as evidence, reiterated however that the monastery had been established by religious women, and that only later on did certain professed brothers come along to support them, and to work in the fields where the women continued to labour, such that the bishop actually gave these women permission to pray outside, in the field or the vineyard, in the event that they were still out there, away from the convent, at the times for prayer.

The life of these female religious devotees in the countryside was certainly neither easy nor safe.

The dangers increased especially from the fourteenth century on, because the Bergamasque political situation had become more uncertain and more violent, with continuous clashes between the Guelphs and the Ghibellines.

So it happened, for example, on the night of Thursday, 2 October 1293, when these Benedictine nuns of Santa Maria di Valmarina were attacked by a group of men who intended to violate the cloister and plunder their convent. When the convent gate was in flames and the guard dog killed, some Ghibellines noticed and came to the defence of the nuns, compelling the assailants to flee. A short time later, this small community decided to move within the walls of the city, where they built a new convent, uniting with other nuns who had also left their primitive rural residences, almost all of which had been founded in the twelfth century.

The same fate befell some communities of Humiliati sisters in the fourteenth century. They had been established in over twenty religious residences in the city and in the Bergamasque territory since the beginning of the thirteenth century. Often undertaking work in the wool trade, the women of this Order had introduced a breath of fresh air into the Lombard religious world. After having been exonerated of an accusation of heresy, they united in double communities, where they lived out their intense evangelical ideal, forerunner to the Franciscan and Dominican experiences, which subsequently would catalyze the interest of faithful laymen and laywomen.

Another context in which the religious exploration of women in the Middle Ages inspired wide-ranging participation is that of hospital care. There were many women who entered hospitals as caregivers. At the time, these places were considered true *loca religiosa* – communities comparable in many ways to convents and monasteries.

But the theme of aid volunteered by women in diverse ways and places, in the home and in the hospital, deserves its very own discussion (and we will speak of it later on) because it represented one of the most pervasive and powerful aspects, although often a hidden one, of female presence not only in the medieval period, but throughout history.

CHAPTER THIRTEEN

GIGLIOLA

AND FASHION

A blue dress with silver buttons, an exquisite tunic above it, the finest bed linen in her trousseau, and a rich dowry.

This is what surrounds Gigliola Suardi when in 1327 she dictates her will, in the beautiful neighbourhood of Canale, situated among the vineyards that face onto the western hills of the city. Gigliola is an aristocrat and she lives like an aristocrat. But not in her own home: for some time she has been the guest of others, being alone, a widow, and childless. She did have a daughter, but death took the child before the mother.

Gigliola was the daughter of Suardo Suardi, and the name Suardi in Bergamo meant something. This ancient lineage was always in charge of the *pars militum* (the faction of nobles of ancient feudal origin), and of the Ghibellines at war against the exiled Guelphs, during the fourteenth century. The leaders of the opposing clan came from the Bonghi family; and Gigliola was given in marriage to Rizzardo Bonghi. A short-lived and strategic agreement between the two families had obviously been at the origin of this marriage that would seem to correspond to the nuptial union between a Montague and a Capulet, beneath the approving gaze of their respective parents, in Shakespearean Verona!

But the marriage between Gigliola and Rizzardo did not lead to any kind of political peace, because the civil war continued; nor to conjugal bliss, seeing as Gigliola does not mention in her will either her husband or her in-laws, a sure sign of animosity.

Gigliola is alone and irate when she uses whatever freedom she has left to decide what to do with her money: besides some donations to the poor (and none to the clerics), she leaves everything to her family of origin. Her legacy goes to her three sisters, to two relatives, and to a friend, as well as to the young children of her daughter, whom she called *Pace* (Peace), a name sadly evocative of the once promising but ultimately failed settlement between the two enemy families, for which the Suardi girl, in turn, had been the sacrificial lamb.

"The suit does not make the man" and neither do wealth and elegance make happiness, as the story of Gigliola seems to suggest. But without underestimating the pain of this unhappy noblewoman, let us turn our attention to her wardrobe and trousseau. It will help us to better understand a relevant aspect of the female world (but not only that) – that of clothing and fashion, which, according to some historians, would have emerged precisely in the fourteenth and fifteenth centuries.

In Gigliola Suardi's will, we find mention of a "*guarnazzone*," or a surcoat (a cloak with enormous sleeves reaching the full length of the garment), typical of the richest of trousseaux. The colour is not specified, nor whether there is or is not a fur lining, as was the custom. Her dress, however, is blue and is decorated with silver buttons: in this case, both the colour and the ornament indicate the high quality of the garment belonging to the Suardi noblewoman.

Let's start with the buttons. Simpler dresses were closed with laces and ribbons, while Gigliola's silver buttons certainly constitute a luxury item, as could belts and pins. In competition with red, blue was one of the most prized and sought-after dyes for clothing and bed linen. In fact, around the thirteenth century we come upon an actual turning-point in the collective mentality regarding the colour blue. It was previously considered a "barbaric" hue. Subsequently it became cherished, in part because the Virgin's mantle was depicted in blue, as were those of the king. The "noble red" would climb the scales of taste once again in the fifteenth century.

Gigliola therefore dressed fashionably. But this was not all. For her bed, she possessed fur blankets and *"de alisto"* coverings as well. This expression comes from the verb *"allistare,"* which means "to create or embellish by means of strips of different type and colour." Gigliola's covers were therefore very fine, with embroidery and inserts of multi-coloured fabrics.

Without reaching the highest extremes of princely glamour, Gigliola Suardi was still a very fine lady, who conformed to Italian and European trends in fourteenth century fashion. It is interesting to note that the styles in dresses and hats reached even distant places, such as Bergamo, a provincial city, via commercial channels, or pictorial art, or through an exchange of news, for instance, about the lavish events taking place in the various courts. In this respect, Milan, with the Visconti family, was already a beacon of taste and trends in the fourteenth century. But Paris itself, so far away, also influenced certain choices in the apparel of the Bergamasque noblewomen, as demonstrated by recent studies on local illuminated manuscripts dating from the thirteenth century.

Before speaking briefly about fashion in broader terms, let us remain a while longer in Bergamasque territory in order to make comparisons with other women, more or less as elegant as Gigliola Suardi. We will do this, as always, on the documentary basis of women's wills, which provide a key to accessing the homes of these women, allowing us to look inside their chests, their closets, and among the furniture, utensils, and those objects left as donations, or sold to acquire money for various purposes.

We will proceed in relation to the representatives of the upper-middle classes and extend our analysis from the clothing to the furniture and even to the household utensils.

Let us start from the bed, which has a strong symbolic, in addition to a commercial, value: it is enough to look at some painted images of the time, containing scenes of childbirth or illness, to remember how the marriage bed is both a place of joy and suffering, of life and death. In this sphere, the iconography of the birth of Mary constitutes one of the most representative examples, with Saint Anne, the mother, in bed, and several servants around her, taking care of the newborn.

For those who were affluent, the bed was a wooden structure, rather wide and tall, often elevated, with a chest underneath or a small step, and a canopy overhead (the latter only for the very rich).

As in Milan and in other cities (but not all), in Bergamo, the bed was the property of the married woman, who thus could dispose of it as she saw fit. Many testatrices donated it for charitable purposes and to benefit their souls. Alberta Bonoldi, for instance, leaves her bed, with related items of her trousseau, to a confraternity that managed a hospice. For the benefit of her soul, she gives another to her brother-in-law, declaring that she received it originally from her mother-in-law. Fantina de Rubeo wishes to give her beds to three hospitals. Franzina Brignoli even decides to have her large bed be divided into four parts, each part to be given to a civic hospital, and the coverings to be sold. She stipulates that, with the earnings from this sale, four wool sheets should be bought to complete the four separate beds. Similarly, other women decide to divide up and donate their beds.

On the same subject of the bedding, some testatrices leave mattresses, quilts, the entire ensemble of coverings and sheets which, depending on the fabric, are called either *linteamina* (of linen) or *cozza* (of wool). Other furniture from the bedroom are coffers, large and small chests, called *scripna* or *scrimniola*, whose literal translation would be "treasure chest," though this does not adequately render the various types of functions that they served. The terms *bancum* and *archebancum* correspond to a writing desk with storage cabinet. The *cadedra* or chair is also donated in these wills, and its mention introduces us to another area in which women work or direct household affairs: the kitchen.

And so pots and pans of various purpose and dimension come to be mentioned in wills: from the *coldera* and its smaller variant *colderola*, the boiler, which was mainly used for doing laundry, to the frying pan, the ladle, or the slotted spoon, to the iron chains used for hanging the cauldron or the earthenware pot for cooking. Small containers for oil or flour are called *regale* or *regiatum*, while the *barenium* is a large chest for storing grain. Stone basins are also donated (*lapideus*), as well as other bowls obviously used for washing things or oneself. In reference to the storage of wine and other liquids, women used and mention in their wills kegs and casks, whose capacities are established on the basis of the *brenta* unit of measurement, which the transporters of wine used and strapped to their shoulders (and thus these people were called *brentatori*). For household illumination, they used lamps fuelled by wax or oil.

The list of all these goods offers a vivid impression of how precious these small objects of ordinary use were in a preindus-trial society, like a wash bowl, for example (in this regard, it is truly interesting to note that, among the miracles attributed to Saint Francis, there is that of having fixed a cracked stone wash bowl, in order to comfort a woman afraid of the angry reaction of her husband!). Second, we observe that during the second half of the fifteenth century (if not indeed in the sixteenth), fur-nishings inside medieval homes were few and essential, and that there were no wardrobes yet (vertical and with doors) as we know them today, but rather trunks and chests.

Ordinary Women

And now let us look at fabrics, dresses, cloaks, hats, and bedding.

The wills of Bergamasque women list fabrics of wool, linen, fustian, twill, and a cloth called *"mesgio"* which could have been made from the knitting together of wool and linen, together with hemp, or from other combinations. Silk does not appear yet. It was predominantly only traded in the area from the late fourteenth century on.

Colours range from the simplest and most humble gray to the most luxurious scarlet, which indicated not only a more costly dye, but also a refined and exquisite fibre. Cloths of blue, green, and a dark brown verging on black or violet were also much-valued. Besides a reference to underwear with the use of the term *"interula"* (a garment to be worn directly on the skin), for the base of female clothing we have the *"socha"* or under-dress, simple garments mostly with long sleeves, over which the women could wear two types of select cloaks: the *"guarnazonum"* (already mentioned for Gigliola Suardi) or the *"cotardita,"* an overcoat often lined in leather. The rich noblewoman Caterina Barzizza lists, for example, a lined *"cotardita de panno morello"* (of dark-brown cloth), and Claradea Gargani, another aristocrat, donates an equivalent item to a priest in order to help him repair the chalice of his church.

Lambswool or sheep's wool is often mentioned and was used either as a lining of a dress or as a bed covering, or as material to fashion a hat: Riccadonna Pelabrocchi, in fact, gives a friend her lambswool hat (*capellum de pelle agni*). More precious furs (sable, ermine, or marten) are not mentioned in Bergamo wills.

These garments could be passed on in good condition or embellished with ornaments (like the already cited buttons) or embroidery (called *frisa*); in this regard, appealingly evocative is the gift of her embroidery tools (*ad frisandum*) that a woman bestows on three girls – everything necessary for the typically female art of embroidery. Other times, clothes have been donated after a prolonged period of use, and therefore a dress may be worn-out, threadbare, or indeed old. It could still be worn by the testatrix, who, in such a case, would specify that. Fantina de Rubeo finds it important to clarify that her *"mesgio"* dress is suitable for the cold season, and she herself used to wear it in winter, and in fact was wearing it at the time of the dictation of her will.

In order to expand our vantage point, and, consequently, to better understand the above-mentioned cases, let us consider briefly some general aspects of medieval feminine apparel. We will do this in reference as well to certain social and symbolic characteristics of clothing.

If, by the twelfth century, certain novel elements have already been introduced into the wardrobe (such as trains, hanging sleeves, and pointed shoes), and a typical predilection for a "verticality" in style, the middle of the fourteenth century marks a turning-point. Women's clothes become more tight-fitting with a tunic, above which a skirt is slit open up to the hips. In wintertime, typical female apparel in the fourteenth century could consist of four or five layers: blouse, skirt, tunic (surcoat), and a fur coat (or lined cloak). From this style of dressing comes the expression "wearing only a skirt" (not being fully dressed), which up until a while ago expressed a more or less sudden impoverishment.

Up until the fourteenth or fifteenth century, the taste for a certain "gracefulness" in the styling of tapered gowns with ample trains, accentuating the effect of verticality, endures, while in the sixteenth, the character of "majesty" asserts itself with a garment consisting of a tight-fitting bodice and a very full skirt. Beneath such skirts, the use of extremely high heels was recommended, such that they became in some cases actual stilts, seeing as their height often reached fifty centimetres! A sixteenth-century example of such exaggerated footwear has been documented in Venice: obviously the women dressed up in this way had to proceed accompanied by someone on either side. The city of lagoons was characterized by its particularly opulent and oriental taste in clothing styles and in the richness of jewels. A curiosity: in Venice the brides wore white, while red together with blue was often preferred by women who were being married elsewhere.

In the fourteenth and fifteenth centuries, progress made in the art of dyeing permitted the wealthier classes to wear clothes in flamboyant colours, indulging a taste that was predisposed towards brighter shades, as Françoise Piponnier remarks:

> The appreciation of colour in contrast to untreated fabrics did not only pertain to the realm of taste: the symbolism of colours permeated the mentality and, by analogy, some apotropaic virtues (the ability to ward off evil) were attributed to certain colours, particularly to red, while yellow had a negative connotation.

For instance, prostitutes in certain cities had to wear small yellow capes to distinguish themselves.

The system of symbols inherited from Antiquity, dominated by the colours red, black, and white, got profoundly altered by the appearance of blue and its derivatives. We have already seen how, dating from the thirteenth century, blue became the preferred colour and was frequently used in the area of clothing, but by the end of the fourteenth century, black, too, met with extraordinary favour in the wealthier environments. And this colour also influenced the choice of darker furs.

The colours of clothes varied also in relation to the stages in life. Green was the hue preferred by the young, especially in clothes to show off during the spring festivals, such as the May

Day celebrations, in which the girls decorated themselves with flower garlands (so well represented in the illuminated manuscripts of the *Tacuina sanitatis* in the Milan of the Visconti era).

During the Italian Renaissance, the revival of classicism brought forth a return to fuller styles in clothing, while the taste for tight-fitting clothing lasted longer in Northern Europe, for example, in the Burgundian court, together with the fashion in pointed footwear and vertical hats: we are dealing with a "Gothic" taste that the new age perceived as outdated. And actually, from the Renaissance on, the centrality of the Italian area as a hub of unique creativity was also reaffirmed within the domain of fashion.

Along with the beauty of clothing, its ostentatious splendour created some moral and political problems, however, which the civic laws tried to regulate with various restrictions. Historians have delved deeply into the significance of the legislation on luxuries, and the assessments in relation to this issue often conflict. There are also divergences in the interpretations of the sermons given by the Franciscan Observants, led by Bernardino da Siena, against excessive opulence in the dress of the rich and the noble. In some cities they even organized a kind of "bonfire of the vanities" with a call to the burning of clothes and luxury ornaments.

If it is true that an excessive moralism sometimes weighs down the sermons of these preachers (with some distasteful misogynist overtones), and if it is also true that the beauty of clothing is an art form (secondary if you will, but real nonetheless, and therefore alive), it was however necessary that some voice be raised to remind the people that, with the price of these clothes, it was possible to feed the poor, who did not wear colourful clothing, and sometimes did not have anything with which to cover themselves at all. Perhaps because she was embittered by her fate as an unhappy wife and lonely mother, not even Gigliola Suardi of Bergamo seems to be aware of the voice of the poor, who receive but a few crumbs in her will, in comparison to all the money earmarked for her illustrious descendants.

And so in her blue gown, both elegant and stylishly decorated, we have before us a model representing the high fashion of the fourteenth century, within which a fragment of a family's prestige is mirrored, but, at the same time, we feel the reverberations of a solitary melancholy.

CHAPTER FOURTEEN

BETTINA

AND HER POTIONS

"Take a fat hen, fill it with cloves, ginger, pepper, saffron, and clear water, and after cooking it, drink its liquid." If this does not work, "prepare a mixture of *marrubium volgare* (white horehound from the mint family) with the testicles of a male hare (dried and then chopped) to take with red wine when going to bed."

This is how Bettina, widow of Zambono Ravizzoni from Gandino, illustrates two remedies she devised to help women who could not produce children. It is 1371 and this healer is practising her vocation in a mountain community, on the side of the Seriana Valley, to the east of Bergamo, in a zone rich in textile production and commerce.

Ten years before, the plague epidemic, which had upset, along with Bergamo, the whole of the Lombardy region, reaping victims in both cities and countryside, had ended. We know that, in Europe, around a quarter of the population died of the contagion, and even if calculations in the Bergamasque area have not yet been made, we can presume that the percentage would not be far off the percentage in other regions. The plague left trepidation in its wake and even changed the way that death was represented. Thus, in Clusone, a populous and lively town not far from Gandino, a fresco of a danse macabre, where death was painted with a skeleton and a scythe, an iconography previously unknown or at least extremely rare, appeared on the walls of a small church.

Despite this, many make the effort to recover from the shock, and among these we have Bettina, who receives patients and advises on remedies even to people from very far away, and in need of her help – such as Giovanni of Brescia, who suddenly lost the ability to speak, and who, after a month being mute, goes to Gandino to get cured. The poor man is told by Bettina to put a well-cooked and still hot chicken on his head. However, beware: the chicken must be a "dove from a nest" and accompanied by other remedies. In fact, it was necessary to boil hyssop (a pungent mint plant), dried wheat, saffron again, and a bunch of daisies, and make of these ingredients a potion that the mute patient must drink. Bettina assures us that with this potion the patient would be cured (perhaps shouting from disgust!).

Another poor "delirious" man (suffering from fever), coming from Crema, is also brought back to health. He had to drink a similar beverage, this time obtained from the boiling of the head of a lamb with the inevitable saffron (Bettina's preferred ingredient), and to place on his head a headdress made with the bones of the same lamb and with some old rope fibres. Within the magical/therapeutic milieu, contact with the bones of the dead, whether animal or human, was considered an effective means to rekindle strength and energy, and bring about healing.

Potions, foods, compresses, movements, postures: the medicinal art (*ars medicinalis*), which Bettina asserts that she has mastered with success, is in fact a practice (*ars* in Latin means "profession") deriving from knowledge of herbal medicine, mixed with archaic and vaguely magical beliefs.

As long as we are dealing with saffron, hyssop, daisies, and horehound, Bettina's procedures seem to fit into that centuries-old tradition of feminine *ars sanitatis* (health care), which, however, in this and other cases, does not reach the more learned level of the books on herbal medicine or the *Tacuina sanitatis* (medieval handbooks on health) which, in the eighth decade of the fourteenth century, would be illuminated, in the Lombard area, by the great Giovannino de Grassi and his workshop. The healer of Gandino is far from the Visconti court where similar texts circulated! Her knowledge comes mostly from an orally transmitted tradition, from woman to woman. There are, among the lists of ingredients she prescribes, medicinal herbs such as horehound and hyssop, both employed for their mucolytic properties in the symptomatic treatment of cough and other benign bronchial conditions.

What is alarming in Bettina's case is rather the characteristic of being able to speak with the dead, something that decidedly transfers her role from that of "healer" to one of "visionary."

There is enough on this subject to linger a while. And so news of Bettina's fame reaches the city of Bergamo, where she is interrogated by the bishop's deputy for some appropriate clarification. Her story has been handed down to us by a testimonial that I published some years ago, on the basis of an eighteenth-century transcription, even if the original is probably still preserved in some notarial repository, as yet undiscovered.

Let us say it right away. Bettina's story has a happy ending. No serious condemnation. Just a recommendation to not continue with suspicious practices, and to stay for a while in the city, under observation, seeing as ten years earlier she was asked to stop, but without any positive result. The woman of Gandino was, in fact, certain of acting for the best. Indeed she states with disarming conviction that those dead who were in contact with her merely asked her to repeat what the Church had been recommending for ages – that one must pay back profit from usury: a moralizing visionary, our Bettina!

Through the course of this questioning, some suspicion of heresy does however emerge with a reference to Friar Dolcino, who had gathered some followers in the Seriana Valley at the beginning of the fourteenth century. On this point as well, Bettina assures the deputy that she is a good Christian and that she has never made the acquaintance of the Dolcinian sect.

There is reason to believe her. At the time of Bettina, it does not seem that the Seriana Valley was a place of refuge or a lure for heretics any longer, whereas there were heretics there between the twelfth and thirteenth centuries, as the story of the Cathar master Giovanni da Lugio (perhaps originally from Vallalta near Albino) suggests. He became bishop of the Cathar church of Desenzano, within which he caused a schism in 1230. Still in the valley, in Albino, twenty followers of Friar Dolcino were condemned to death in 1329.

The heresy theme in Bergamo should be re-examined in the light of the most recent historiography; the presumed or real heterodox inclination often attributed to Bergamasque citizens (traditionally pro-imperial in the era of the Communes) is configured more as a political alignment than as an actual deeply rooted religious choice. Only in 1267, for example, did the Orobic Commune introduce norms against heresy within the statutes: much later than other cities.

One motive, which limited the consolidation of heretical communities in the area whose presence up to that point was undeniable and verified, was also the early and widespread introduction into the Bergamasque territory of evangelical "orthodox" groups (or ones that reverted to orthodoxy), such as the members of the Humiliati movement, made up of men and women who lived in communities or who remained within their families, following the ideals of a broader fraternity. They adopted a lifestyle which attracted, in particular, those lay brothers desirous of following the Christian experience with renewed conviction. After having obtained from Pope Innocent III the surprising permission to give oral sermons, at least of a moral if not a theological nature, the Humiliati lay brothers spread throughout not only the city but also the medieval Lombardy countryside, often founding small double communities (male and female), in which they prayed and worked, according to ancient Benedictine principles, but with a sensibility that I would call "pre-Franciscan." Often, with the earnings from their textile work, they donated clothing of rough wool to the poor; they cultivated fields that they generally leased and did not own, according to an initial and strong evangelical-pauperist inspiration. Where their communities were established, there is noticeably less of a need to follow other movements external to the Catholic Church.

So it was in Bergamo, with around twenty Humiliati foundations which sprang up in the city, but mostly in the country, between the end of the twelfth century and the first half of the thirteenth, a period that marks the maximum expansion of the movement, which would later pass the baton to the Mendicant Orders and the lay confraternities. It does not seem to be an accident that the establishment of the Humiliati coincided with the progressive phasing out of the heretical movement.

This does not mean, as already mentioned, a denial of the presence of heretics in the Bergamo area, confirmed also by some papal documents of the early thirteenth century, and by the earliest possible introduction of the friars of the Order of Preachers into the diocese (the summer of 1220): besides the above-mentioned Cathars and Dolcinians, for the history of heresy in Bergamo, the most famous episode remains that of the Waldensian convention held in the city in May of 1218 between a group of Poveri Lombardi (calling themselves *fratres Ytalici*) and the Poveri di Lione (called Ultramontani).

Afterwards there is silence on the subject up until the period between the thirteenth and fourteenth centuries, when, even in

Bergamo, the activity of inquisitors begins. Besides the already mentioned case of Albino, death sentences are not documented in this period, but the heretics were impeded by financial punishment. Fines for heresy involved some women; the charges increased in the first two decades of the fourteenth century, also involving two "orthodox" religious communities, the female Humiliati of Osio and the female Augustinians of San Giorgio in Redona. In both cases, it concerns convents in extreme crisis, overwhelmed by the endemic state of war that, among other things, made it difficult to oversee land management. Rather than being heretics, these women were deeply in debt!

Going back to Bettina and the accusation of heresy, during the 1371 interrogation, the question on witchcraft, a term which above all meant the improper or indeed sacrilegious use of the Eucharistic Bread, could have been the most pernicious. In 1304, the bishop of Bergamo, Giovanni da Scanzo, had already spoken out against the theft and malicious use of the consecrated host. He categorically forbade the use of the Body of the Lord, consecrated wine, and holy oil in order to concoct magic spells, potions, "incantations," or medications to heal various illnesses, or for other reasons.

The phenomenon therefore existed, here as elsewhere, but our widow of Gandino declares all this to be unrelated to her. She admits, on the other hand, to having much success with the women who turned to her for problems connected mostly with family life.

Bettina's "style" reminds us of another playful (if not humorous) episode that took place in Bergamo in the sixteenth century: some wives, in order to resolve marital conflicts, put into their husbands' soup some dust scraped from the statues of Adam and Eve, situated near the entrance to the Basilica of Sant'Alessandro in the Upper City. The originality of this specific case is not so much in the practice of iconophagia (the eating of icons), quite common everywhere in Christian Europe, especially in relation to Marian images, but particularly in the choice of figures, referring to the biblical progenitors, to the first husband and wife couple.

The trial of these women, surprised in the act of "scraping," ended in the seizure of the dust and a simple reprimand.

The story of Bettina from Gandino has led us onto the trail of numerous female healers in search of remedies, healers that are sometimes fantasists or easily suggestible, other times widely active in the area of domestic cures, treating various ills, basically, with the means available to them.

CHAPTER FIFTEEN

MARGHERITA

AND CARE-GIVING

Who knows whether "our" Margherita would have known the story of other women of the same name, ones who were recognized – for good or bad – as important and famous figures between the thirteenth and fourteenth centuries?

For instance, there was Margherita da Cortona, the beautiful Margherita of the Perugia countryside. She became the lover of a country nobleman, who, however, was assassinated without having married her, leaving her alone with a son of around nine. She was not just beautiful; she was also courageous. Margherita went to Cortona and won back her reputation. She helped women in labour, founded a hospital, and became a Franciscan tertiary, as well as an urban hermit. Many came to her for advice – to such an extent that the ex-mistress ended her days, in 1297, surrounded by an aura of sanctity.

We also know about the young Margherita of Ypres, who, mostly inside her home, lived an apparently banal life but with surprising results: this girl, who died when she was about twenty in 1237, was considered blessed for her fresh sense of innocence, making her, *ante litteram* of course, a sort of little Thérèse. Simply speaking, she was a lover of the Lord, and without any grand gestures, sat at the feet of whoever was reading the Bible to her, like the evangelical sister of Lazarus who chose the "best part." It was described in this way by Thomas of Cantimpré, a Dominican, decidedly more gracious and honest than his colleagues, who, in Paris, in 1310, considered heretical another Margherita – Margherita Porete. They condemned her to be burned at the stake because she was not willing to disavow her own ideas.

The story of our Margherita has an important word in common with these other stories, a word which can be said without the fear of sounding sentimental, because it is a word that sometimes demands much pain, even the shedding of blood: this is the word love.

Love for a man, love for God, love for intellectual freedom, as evidenced by the three above-mentioned Margheritas, and love for one's own family, in need of treatment and care, demonstrated by Margherita de Pillis, who lived in Bergamo at the end of the fourteenth century.

It is April of 1399, and the air reeks of war.

The Guelphs and the Ghibellines are killing each other in continual ambushes and incursions that reach into the heart of the city's boroughs. Rival families promise peace, and then they resume slaughtering each other. One poor pregnant woman, searching in the fields for medicinal herbs, is even butchered by some armed rabble: we deduce this from the chronicles of the time (Tarussi, Castelli), steeped in tragedies, in which men do not know how to free themselves of the fierce logic of blood feuds, family misfortunes, and natural disasters.

It is within this context that the story of Margherita de Pillis appears even more glowing. She was a member of an affluent notarial family who lived in the rich Arena neighbourhood, and possessed a castle, as well, to the north of the city, in charming Valmarina. The de Pillis family, in the thirteenth century, had supported the birth of the local Misericordia Confraternity and, in the following century, they seem to orient themselves politically towards the Ghibellines. In a 1399 document which remembers her, Margherita is distinguished as a *domina*, namely a "lady," an appellation attributed to women of the upper-middle class.

After marrying Bertolamino Zucchi, the son of a merchant, Margherita lives well-protected, in the heart of the Upper City, not far from her house of origin, near the Basilica of Santa Maria Maggiore, in a dwelling well-provided with outer walls, a tiled roof, a courtyard, a vegetable garden, and many bedrooms with comfortable beds. Her sickly husband, however, is lying in one of these rooms. Margherita is taking care of him, not neglecting, all the same, their two daughters, Giovannina and Antoniola.

These scenes of domestic life occur beneath the gaze of the mother-in-law, Femminina de Vazzio, who is aware of the fact that her daughter-in-law has behaved and still behaves admirably, and this fact is noteworthy. She recognizes this with words and actions, as evidenced in her will, in which she stipulates for Margherita not only the legitimate restitution of her dowry, but also a sizeable additional bequest with the following reasoning: "For the love and loyalty which she bore and continues to bear towards the above-named Femminina, to her daughters [those of Margherita and Bertolamino] and which she bore towards Bertolamino, once her husband, during his long illness, which he contracted and endured."

Thus we are given a glimpse of family life, in which the young Margherita tended to her infirm husband (for an unspecified but extended period of time), who eventually died, and also lovingly looked after her mother-in-law and her children.

The elderly woman, who reserves sweet words of sincere gratitude for her daughter-in-law, was not a docile type. Actually she was a decisive and combative woman in asserting herself before her antagonists, because she had to defend her rights against the relatives of her husband, who laid claim to part of her assets. (The fourteenth-century Zucchi family, I regret to say, did not behave well towards the brides who married into their clan. Earlier, in 1335, Benvenuta de Poma, wife of Graziadeo Zucchi, had complained to her husband about the non-fulfillment of the promised *morgengabe* and, once her spouse died, lashed out against her son for not respecting the deal either. And so she saved the receipt of the promised gifts for more than a half-century and, producing it when she was drafting her will, she left nothing to the Zucchi family, reserving every legacy to her family of origin!)

Femminina de Vazzio had therefore undertaken a court case against her in-laws, one in which she was aided by a certain Giorgio, a Bergamo citizen, who benefits from her last will and testament, with a generous and plentiful quantity of wine. They would surely have toasted all together, after the successful outcome of the trial.

With justice re-established, Femminina makes an important gesture: she names as universal heirs the poor of Bergamo, after having allocated a legacy for the association in charge of financial maintenance and restorations to Santa Maria Maggiore. The gift is substantial because she donates the house in which she is living, in the extremely central Antescolis neighbourhood, guaranteeing however the usufruct, or the legal right to enjoy the profits of her property, to her daughter-in-law Margherita and her grand-daughters, until these latter marry or enter a convent. From these last words we can deduce that in 1399 Margherita's daughters were still under age, and that their mother must have still been quite young at the time of the drafting of Femminina's will.

Without the words of this lively mother-in-law, who knew how to defend herself from the rich and benefit the poor, we would know nothing about Margherita, whose decency and generosity would have remained hidden behind the domestic walls of a beautiful Bergamasque home at the end of the fourteenth century.

Margherita's little story opens a window also onto the larger theme of daily life, into its aspects of mentality, of religiosity, of the transmission of values. Can an historian enter into the house of a medieval woman, not only to peek at her furniture and clothes (as we have done with Gigliola Suardi), but also to uncover behaviours and even the feelings of individuals? And can this historian ask about what and who might have influenced certain conscious actions, such as the generosity of spirit demonstrated by Margherita? I believe so.

In this case, for instance, besides the influence absorbed through family (from mother to daughter), we know that some laywomen kept and read the Psalter in their home (there is a case documented in Bergamo in 1259), or they listened to a "specialized" form of sermon, one addressed exclusively to them, and in which the family is presented more and more "in their positive opportunities for salvation" (Del Corno). The study of images and sacred objects, found in private dwellings (and often cited in wills), also constitutes a useful path towards outlining characteristics of what has been aptly defined as "domestic religion." And finally, the iconographic analysis of particular moments of family life, recognizable in frescoes of both sacred and profane subject matter, is highly indicative of situations that could take place behind domestic walls, as demonstrated in an extremely beautiful fourteenth-century fresco (of Bergamasque origin) depicting a visit of two doctors to a sick patient, lying in a large and elegant bed. With a sad expression, a woman lightly pulls aside a corner of a drape hanging from the canopy of the bed, and looks at the viewer of the painting, allowing him/her to observe the scene in a discreet manner. This seems to be the exact image of the story that we have been narrating here.

What Margherita de Pillis did at home for her husband testifies to how daily life can take on a heroic quality.

Inasmuch as a woman of her means would certainly have servants to help in the nursing of her husband, to stay for so long in such close proximity to illness demands a great deal. And Margherita did it with love and devotion: an attitude not to be taken for granted – then as now.

Now we would like to provide a name and some features to other women who also cared for others, but outside of the home. We will do this once again in relation to a specific reality – Bergamo – knowing full well, however, that this reality also reflects perspectives and mentalities that are wider and more general. We will speak therefore about women who entered hospitalier houses, about women who were paid for their nursing, and also about others who were volunteer collaborators in this variegated world of health care.

An acute observer of thirteenth-century religious reality, Giacomo da Vitry, stated that it was necessary to have the courage of a martyr to overcome the repulsion inspired by the filth of sick patients. And yet many men and women founded hospitals or voluntarily entered into service of the sick and the invalid, especially in the twelfth and thirteenth centuries, centuries that were characterized by a real "revolution in Charity."

Entering a hospitalier house as a caregiver corresponded in many ways to entry into a convent, in the sense that hospitals were considered religious places, and a profession of vows was therefore required. The caregivers of the sick were called lay brothers/sisters and their superiors were called minister.

The presence of many active women is noticeable in Bergamo's hospitals, which – for the sake of clarity – I will now group into three distinct categories: mixed hospitals, women's hospitals, and family hospitals. The Hospital of Santa Maria della Carità in Borgo Canale, for instance, belonged to the first group. It was founded in the twelfth century by a layman, Landolfo della Crotta, with the collaboration of the canons of Sant'Alessandro. In this hospice the poor, the infirm, and pilgrims were received, according to the criterion of multifunctionality, which was a typical characteristic of the smaller care facilities of the era. A small group of lay brothers and sisters – never more than about ten – worked for around half a century in the Landolfo house, until in 1230, the first of Bergamo's Friars Minor, who cooperated with their allies in health care, took up residence in this same hospital. From 1277, the Poor Clares, replacing the Friars who moved elsewhere, continued to do the same.

In the twelfth century, the majority of Bergamo's small hospitals, likewise, did not belong to the hospitalier orders, but were founded by laypersons, supported by the bishop. This was the case as well for the leprosarium of San Lazzaro, for which a kind of "co-management" of the property, shared among the patients and their caregivers, has been confirmed. The treatment of lepers was perceived as a particularly heroic activity in the Middle Ages, given the deep-seated disgust this disease engendered. It was in Bergamo, sometime around the last decade of the twelfth century, that some members of the citizen management class entered as caregivers into the San Lazzaro house, marking a radical turning-point in their life, in keeping with the characteristics of some famous conversions, in many ways similar to that of Saint Francis of Assisi. Women, on the other hand, were not active among the caregivers of Bergamo's leprosarium. This was not the case in other cities, such as Verona, famous for that most beautiful story of the widow Garscenda, who built a small house in which to nurse "her" leper, declaring that she had made this choice for love of God and her husband. Her example was later followed by others.

If not present within the community of laypersons, Berga-masque women nevertheless aided the San Lazzaro leprosarium through numerous donations, showing their preference for this hospital, together with the above-mentioned Hospital of Santa Maria della Carità, and the Crociferi Hospital that took in orphans.

From the thirteenth century on, but especially in the four-teenth century, other caregiving structures were operated exclu-sively by women: such were the hospices attached to two female Dominican convents (Mater Domini and Santa Marta) and one run by Augustinians (Santa Margherita in Pignolo), the parish hospice of Santa Caterina, the mountain hospital of Clusone, the rural one of Stezzano (established by a canon with the help of a rich widow), and a civic hospital founded by another canon at the Cathedral of San Vincenzo, and then managed for a long time by two women, responsible for its administration in its totality.

Another interesting circumstance is that of hospitals being set up through family initiatives. In 1336, for instance, in Val Brembana, Zambono Carrara obtains permission from Berga-mo's bishop to use his assets to establish a hospital in Lepreno in order to welcome, feed, and treat the ill there; whatever would carry forward from the financial budget of the hospital would be distributed to the poor. What is especially significant, in terms of our theme, is a passage from the decree of foundation, in which Zambono states that the Lepreno Hospital must have a male minister and a female minister, six counsellors, and several caregivers, male and female; he therefore asks the bishop if he could become the minister together with his wife Giovanna, who would work alongside him in the role of female minister, while their daughter Giacoma would be "*soror ad administrandum et de-serviendum infirmis*," in other words, someone who would dedicate herself to the service of the sick. Husband, wife, and daughter are therefore the founders and earliest protagonists in a health care initiative far from the city, in a mountain region, substantiating how certain ideals spread further afield into rural areas and down into the valley as well.

Besides their presence in hospitals, women were very active in collaborating with other charity institutions, such as the Misericordia Maggiore Confraternity in Bergamo. Even though they might not have played leadership roles, the female registrants of the Misericordia supported the confraternity with donations, which in specific periods even reached extremely substantial amounts (from a quarter to a half of total aid), and participated in the distribution of charity, in the preparation of food to deliver within the various neighbourhoods, in the recommendation of cases of need, and in the fostering of minors.

It has been documented, on this subject, that salaried helpers in the capacity of nannies or nursemaids were being hired on the part of the Misericordia.

Nannies paid by the Confraternity included Marchina, Bruna, and Bona in 1362, and an anonymous woman was recorded as nursemaid to an invalid, and remunerated with 5 coins by the Misericordia for many days of care to a sick patient (in the same period, the salary and the duration of their assignment for two male carers have been specified, and because of this we can determine – with all due caution, and in the hope of not horrifying the specialists – a monthly salary corresponding to 300 of our current euros, plus room and board).

To these "helping professionals" can be added the private servants that were paid to carry out diverse tasks, in which, besides cleaning, cooking, and other services, was included the care of children, the elderly, and the sick, as members of the family group.

Elsewhere (chapter 10) we named some of these servants: they were those registered in the Misericordia Confraternity.

Among these, a certain Margherita was mentioned, without any other designations: no surname, nor the title of *domina*, with which instead Margherita de Pillis was defined – the young mother and widow with whom we began.

And yet even the extremely unknown servant Margherita, together with so many others, belongs, as a fully fledged member, to the history of generosity and charity, which is perhaps one of the most beautiful stories that could ever be told.

CHAPTER SIXTEEN

BELFIORE

ON THE ROAD

Belfiore stands and beholds the line of the Appenines that stretches out over the distant horizon, on a clear day in April, after the wind has cleansed the sky, and from the hills of Upper Bergamo, this panorama sweeps over the entire plain.

It is the spring of 1350 and many are going to Rome for the Jubilee: can a woman like her – a childless widow, perhaps not so young – brave such a trip and risk, among other things, contagion from the plague, which has been harvesting victims in central Italy for over two years, while her city has remained immune from it? Moreover, the pope is no longer in Rome; he's in Avignon, having left Rome in squalor and subject to the discord between the dominant and domineering factions of the times.

Belfiore knows what she is risking, but she wants to defy the dangers and states it officially, dictating, before witnesses and a notary, these precise words in the third person: "*vult ire ad Romam*" ("she wants to go to Rome") to revisit the places where the bodies of Peter and Paul and other saints, male and female, are located. In the Latin of the text, in fact, there is no use of the term "tombs," but rather of "bodies," with an incisive reference to the perception that pilgrims saw themselves as coming into contact with the "living"; it is not clear, on the other hand, if the term "*ad rivisitandum*" refers to a previous pilgrimage already undertaken by this testatrix, or to the habit of visiting and travelling between the various stages and stations of which the Jubilee programme consisted. In any case, in 1350, this brave woman wants to become a "*Romea*," the pilgrim who goes to Rome.

All these reports are contained in Belfiore's will, where we read that, before leaving and after having named her brother her heir, in the absence of any other close relatives, she specifies a substantial donation, so that a large cross may be sculpted, and painted, and then placed above the altar of Santa Maria Maggiore, the city's most beautiful church, a majestic architectural complex dating back to the twelfth century, which during this particular period was being adorned with statues, frescoes, and various wooden structures. Today the crucifix is still hanging where Belfiore requested it to be, but who could have imagined that among the sponsors of this work there was also a pilgrim?

This has been revealed to us by her will, often the best source for learning the identity of this woman and other medieval women on the road – especially the less famous ones, travelling during the late Middle Ages, and not leaving behind any letters, reports, diaries, or other evidence.

And perhaps it is not coincidental that one of the most studied Italian regions, the Veneto region, from the point of view of women's wills, is also the area that presents us with the most evocative representatives of "humble female pilgrims." Their stories emerge thanks to the person who had the patience to dig into the archives, among thousands of parchments, in order to find "first-hand stories," such as the one regarding four Veronese women about to leave for the Holy Land in 1410. Besides Rome and Santiago de Compostela, Jerusalem prevailed, in fact, as the most desirable destination for over a millennium, even if the journey to reach it was decidedly the most dangerous, the most costly, and the longest, since it lasted on the average about seven or eight months.

Agnese, Giuliana, Caterina, and Romana (the last one perhaps a daughter of a *Romea* – a pilgrim to Rome?) are the members of the group from Verona. These women of average or little social and economic importance, all widows, seem conscious of the risks they have to undergo, to the extent that one of them explicitly hints at the possibility of not coming back alive. Before leaving, they make donations of money to the poor – in two cases designated as universal heirs – highlighting that they mean actual vagabonds, the truly needy, deprived of any means of protection. Giuliana moreover leaves her silk tunic to the image of the Virgin venerated by the confraternity in which she is registered. Such arrangements are evidence of both the profound awareness of the decision taken, and the characteristics of a spirituality attentive to the reality of the most destitute.

Similar interest characterizes the will of another pilgrim from Verona, Margherita, who, on the verge of leaving to visit the "Holy Sepulchre of our Lord" in 1414, names as her heirs, in the second instance, the poor (both men and women), after having guaranteed the use of her house (in her absence) to a priest friend, with whom she had also previously shared the adoption of a girl – defined as a "soul daughter" – who bore the same name: Margherita.

Still in the Venetian region, this time in the city of Treviso, it is notable that the number of women exceeds that of men in the direct overseas pilgrimages during the years 1350–1450. Treviso was an important city in the network of pilgrimages, especially for those who, from Northern Europe, wished to reach Rome, or to embark in Venice, in order to set sail in turn for Middle Eastern ports, after having stopped in various locations. In the fourteenth and fifteenth centuries, the city of Saint Mark's represented, in fact, the principal port of embarkation for the

Holy Land, to the extent that a regular "shipping service" had been organized for the transportation of pilgrims, who were greeted by actual travel managers, ready to offer and negotiate prices, services, and routes. The wait times for departure could last, however, for weeks, and that affected costs and the entire length of the crossing.

And it is precisely in the Venetian documentation that a text of great interest, about women's participation on pilgrimages to Palestine, has been discovered. Giampaolo Cagnin describes it as:

> a resolution of the Venetian senate on July 5, 1384, with respect to permission to travel to the Holy Land, one that we could define as organized on a city or diocese basis, granted to a group of pilgrims from Urbino, departing from Pesaro: out of thirty departing pilgrims, twenty are women. Furthermore, on this trip, even three Jews were taken on board, with their wives, and two girls (probably they were also on pilgrimage to their holy city) and another twenty persons to board in Venice.

The Venetian galleys left in turn for Beirut, from where the pilgrims could proceed by sea to Jaffa, and then continue on foot towards Jerusalem.

This itinerary was probably also followed by the Venetian Lucia da l'Asedo, who in 1384 dictated her will as she was about to leave for the Church of the Holy Sepulchre. In her case, besides endowments to the clergy and the poor, it is very interesting to point out that this pilgrim declares to be carrying with her a breviary, lent to her by a friar friend. This is not an isolated case (we will speak of it shortly) and testifies to the awareness and depth of conviction with which these women prepared to travel.

The Venetian documentation furthermore highlights the charity institutions as well, which, here as elsewhere, hosted the pilgrims in transit or those who were sick. Hospices and hostels often functioned as banks to guarantee the necessary means of return, as demonstrated by the lists of deposits in money made to this end at the Treviso hospice. We find here the name of some women coming from Germany; one of them, Caterina, is not able to depart because she dies during her hospitalization here, and it is poignant to note how she had left, in her "purse," the necessary money to cover the expenses of her treatment, and her possible burial.

Someone who attends the funeral of a travelling pilgrim – and he describes it in great detail – is that scholarly, gossipy, and eccentric humanist, Giovanni Conversini, who, in 1400, tells in his *Rationarum Vitae* about an adventurous diplomatic mission to Rome, on the return from which he crossed paths with a group of pilgrims, who were burying a woman who died on the way. It is a brief and touching testament about an unknown pilgrim, towards whom her fellow-travellers show affection and feel a sense of nostalgia. During pilgrimages, friendships could develop (then as now).

Returning again to wills, and more generally to notarial sources, other cases of women pilgrims emerge in Ligurian archives. Similar, in certain aspects, to the story of Belfiore, our pilgrim to Rome departing from Bergamo, is the story of Simona Doria, who in 1212 leaves Genoa on the way to Rome, and draws up a will rich in pious bequests, of which one is destined to the acquisition of a chalice for an ill-equipped church. And even earlier, around the end of the twelfth century, a widow named Gisla had made her solemn profession of vows to the Canons Regular of the Holy Cross of Mortara, in Paverano, after having returned from a pilgrimage in Galicia. The same provostry of

Mortara was born because of endowments and wills drawn up along the Compostela itineraries, as Valeria Polonio notes:

> The Canons of Mortara in the Genoa area are often involved with pilgrims: those who are about to leave remember them in their wills or even draw up a deed in one of their houses ... specifically speaking, the clerics of Paverano take custody of the estate of another pilgrim, Giuliana, who is also heading towards Santiago de Compostela.

Furthermore, the ladies who made their money and jewels available for the crusade, at the beginning of the fourteenth century, proposing, as well, their personal participation, hailed from the Genoa region. In truth, their armed pilgrimage, even though it was praised for its purpose, never took place, and therefore the women never left, but the fact of their proposal, in itself, is very significant. The episode has been recreated by the same Polonio on the basis of two letters of Pope Boniface VIII:

> The famous "women's crusade" dates back to the autumn of 1301: in response to fresh Islamic successes in the near East and to the inefficiency of every counteraction (the fall of St. John of Acre took place in 1292), a group of upper-class women makes an offer to the Pope to arm a fleet at their expense; one of them is even ready to set off, but with a realistic plan of financial support – a far cry from mere wishful thinking. Those that submit the proposal to the Pope, however, belong to families on the opposing side. The initiative is explicitly religious and, one could say, offered in expiation for the recent actions connected to interdictions and for the blood and devastation caused by internal struggles. But it is quickly juxtaposed by a programme (not put forth by the women) of reconstruction,

to the advantage of Genoa, of Tripoli in Mamluk Syria;
Boniface VIII, fearful of possible rivalries between
Christians in the East, declares a halt to the crusade. This
beautiful, promising, much-praised project dissolves
into nothing.

Moving on from the Venetian and Ligurian (Genoa) regions
to another Italian region, Tuscany, documentation proves varied and includes a chronicle-type and hagiographic narrative
vein, which can offer, with the necessary interpretive caution,
interesting information on the thousand-year-old tradition of
female pilgrimages.

And so from the lives of saints or the blessed emerge many
stories of Tuscan women, connected in diverse ways to the vast
world of religious itinerancy, between the twelfth and thirteenth
centuries, as Anna Benvenuti explains:

It is in this period, for example, that the sources attest
to a unique flowering of both trends throughout Tuscia
crossed by the Via Francigena (the ancient pilgrimage
route to Rome): that of the real pilgrimage of women
and that of the symbolic pilgrimage, experienced through
either voluntary reclusion as the final phase of the itinerant experience, or with active care of the sick within the
hospital structures along the way.

Let us look at some examples. Cristiana da Santa Croce became the lady-in-waiting of a devout, penitent matron, accom-
panying her on the Apulian pilgrimage route to the Sanctuary of
Monte Sant'Angelo; Bona from Pisa went to Jerusalem to seek
her biological father, who had abandoned her as a child, and
ultimately found the footsteps of the Heavenly Father in the imitation of the life of the Anchorite saints of the Thebaid; other

women would travel along the roads, seeking environments appropriate for the creation of regular religious communities: it is enough to mention the names of Saint Humility from Faenza or that of the Blessed Sperandea among the many examples.

There is someone who stands out among the Tuscan pilgrims of the fifteenth century – Eugenia, a nun of a strict enclosed order, who leaves the cloister, reaches Rome, and then goes on to Jerusalem, where she settles down in service to a hospice, and then departs for Compostela in Galicia, to ultimately return to the convent in Florence from which she originally set out, and into which she was again received. Her adventurous story, outlined in a sixteenth-century chronicle, has been recently confirmed in its historicity by a rich series of letters in the archive of the Florentine Murate (the home of these *murate* or "walled-in" nuns), in particular in the folder that goes from August 1488 to November 1503.

The "pilgrim nun" is a contradiction from an institutional perspective, because convent life calls for a commitment to *stabilitas* (stability) and the argument against travelling nuns and monks represented a veritable controversy within medieval Christianity, even during the times when the call to set out for Palestine resounded most strongly. We need only remember that, up until Bernard de Clairvaux designed the Rule for the Knights Templar in the twelfth century, the figure of the monk-warrior had caused considerable concern.

For this reason, the story of Eugenia is surprising, since she went from her status as a nun to that of a Franciscan tertiary, and as such, provided assistance to pilgrims in Jerusalem for nearly thirty years. In this Jerusalem period, and during the course of other journeys, Eugenia even forged ties with the courts of Spain and Portugal, and also with "an interesting constellation of women who, at various times, stayed in Jerusalem, and afterwards, maintained a filial relationship of friendship and veneration with the Pilgrim" (Zarri).

A point of reference for the Tuscan women in Jerusalem was the Hospice of Mount Zion, annexed to the Franciscans' hospice, and founded in 1354 by another Florentine woman, Sofia di Filippo degli Arcangeli; in this building, there were 200 beds which could accommodate poor persons and pilgrims, cared for by women who deserved their reputation for holiness among Christians, as well as the respect of Muslims, as demonstrated in a tract from 1485, written by Francesco Suriano:

> These "*Bizoche*" [religious laywomen], to the confusion of wicked and sinful Christians, are much-honoured and favoured in the city or the countryside. And this reverence is generally offered to all the women, whether they be Christians, Jews, or Muslims. And for this reason, these *Bizoche* move securely in the Judean Hills, Bethany, and Bethlehem, and throughout the city, without a guide or companion.

From the same source, we know, among other things, that the flow of women pilgrims into the Holy City was notable because the role of the "*bizoche*" was not so much to serve the Friars Minor, but to "receive the women pilgrims that continually come to Jerusalem" (Suriano).

The description of the peaceful coexistence among the women in a land torn apart by conflicts (then as now) is certainly moving!

The experience of the female religious community, active near the Hospice of Mount Zion, confirms moreover the continuity of the pilgrimage tradition to the Holy Land, by women of humble social status who, freed of family obligations, dedicated some years of their life to the service of others who came to see the holy sites. They may have been socially humble but they were not uneducated, given that the ownership of books is documented by some of them: in fact, Eugenia, like the above-mentioned Lucia, also possessed a breviary, from which she reluctantly separated herself at the moment she left Jerusalem to go to Compostela.

Eugenia's case additionally shows us that the chronicles and epistolary sources offer a wealth of particulars on the mentality and stories of the women pilgrims, that last wills and testaments (obviously) cannot, at least not in such a richly detailed way. Letters, chronicles, and trip diaries are, however, generally, available only in reference to pilgrimages by women of a certain fame and prestige, as we have already seen in the case of Bridget of Sweden, in the first part of this book.

And precisely the remembrance of the Swedish princess-prophet generates a final question: who knows whether Bridget encountered Belfiore, the Rome pilgrim, with whom we began our story? In 1350, both of them might have stood side by side in Rome, among the people flocking there for the Jubilee.

This meeting, however, remains unknown to us, but it certainly is a pleasure to fantasize it.

IN AN EFFORT NOT TO CONCLUDE ...

> I also ask you to bring me those sweetmeats which you
> used to give me when I was ill in Rome.

The person speaking is a man who has chosen poverty as a lifestyle, and who addresses a rich – very rich – woman. The two are
friends. Indeed, these simple words sound like a declaration of
friendship between a man and a woman, and are truly beautiful.
We find ourselves confronted by a "fragment of mutual tender-
ness" between two interlocutors who are extremely well-known
to each other, and who can limit themselves to essentials, without adding anything further, also because there is little time left:
"Sister Death" is about to make her appearance.

 Let us look at the context of the above-mentioned words, by
setting forth, in full, the short letter that contains them. It was
dictated by Francis of Assisi for a Roman noblewoman, Jacopa
dei Settesogli, a few days before 4 October 1226:

> Brother Francis, the poor man of Christ, wishes Lady
> Jacopa, the servant of the Most High, health in the Lord
> and communion in the Holy Ghost. Dearest, I want you
> to know that the blessed Lord has done me the grace of
> revealing that the end of my life is nigh. So, if you want
> to find me still alive, hurry here to Santa Maria degli
> Angeli as soon as you receive this letter. Because if you get
> here later than Saturday, you might not see me alive. And
> bring with you an ash-coloured cloth to wrap my body in,
> and the candles for the burial. I also ask you to bring me

those sweetmeats which you used to give me when I was
ill in Rome.

It is a sign of fondness and intimate familiarity, the decision of
who should take care of one's own body after death. And Francis chooses a woman for this task. He would wish to die "naked
on the naked earth," but for his funeral, he entrusts himself to
Jacopa, who loves him and has been following him for a long
time, perhaps since 1209, when he went to Rome to request
Pope Innocent III's approval for the first brotherhood.

Married, mother of two sons, widowed early on, Jacopa remained faithful to Francis even in subsequent years, as that explicit reference to her having tended to a sick man in need of
care suggests. The two were probably of the same age and, having
become friends in life, are now buried beside each other, in the
crypt of the Basilica of St Francis of Assisi.

Jacopa would arrive in time at Porziuncola, in those first days
of October 1226, and would enshroud the body of her friend,
after having embraced him, just like the Magdalene did with
Christ.

With Francis's brief letter to Lady Jacopa dei Settesogli, we
are not encountering a text structured with ascetic-hagiographic
concerns in mind: this is borne out by the letter's finishing
touch – that exceedingly authentic reference to the sweetmeats,
which another Franciscan source (the *Compilatio Assisiensis*) explains are that dessert which the Romans call "*mostaccioli*" and are
made with almonds, sugar, honey, and other ingredients.

Francis knew about good and beautiful things: he also openly
stated it in the Canticle of Brother Sun, in which he praised
God through His creatures, including the "bright stars," perhaps an allusion to Clare's eyes, and other good things, such as
his friendship with Jacopa.

Whoever loves created reality, also loves (or should love) women and what they know how to make, including cookies. It should not surprise us that this declaration of love comes from a man who endured so many sacrifices in his life: he "simply" wished to follow in Jesus' footsteps, and in the Gospel, one can read that the Lord accepted to sit at the table, and savour the wine, bread, and other good things. They even accused him of being a drunkard, a table companion of sinners and prostitutes ("Here is a glutton and a drunkard, a friend of tax collectors and sinners," Matthew 11:19):

It was Jesus himself who referred to the disparaging portrait that was being disseminated about him: a destiny which in some ways even touched Francis of Assisi, both in the sappy caricatures of certain films, and in the accusation of a presumed misogyny found in some critical essays.

But the short note sent to Lady Jacopa persuades us more than such interpretations.

The sensitivity, the affection, the underlying reasons behind this episode of friendship between a man and a woman are evidence of a broader story, which precedes the year 1226, dating back – as has been noted – to the origins of Christianity.

At the heart of the Christian message we have, in fact, the Incarnation, and – pardon my fundamental but not simplistic premise – if God became incarnate, it means that reality (material and corporeal) is "good," beginning with the uterus of that woman who was His mother.

The drama of evil is also present in this "good reality," but not in the dualistic terms that certain schools of thought have represented it, inside and outside the official Church, during the Middle Ages. Some moralist clerics, who despised women and preached against the body and sexuality from church pulpits, were dualists; but so were those Cathar heretics who proclaimed, in different terms, that there was a distinct separation between body and soul, stating that a god of evil had created matter.

The best response to the Cathar provocation, which in the twelfth and thirteenth centuries caused a crisis in the Church of Rome, was obviously not the heinous persecution that martyred religious dissidence, but rather the experience, often silent and hidden, of those who remained faithful to the original nucleus of the Christian message, which, to all intents and purposes (albeit taking into consideration precise details and nuances), effectively represented a characteristic feature of the medieval period. It is appropriate to reiterate this, without confessional and anachronistic pretences of historiographic hegemony.

This line of thinking – faithful to the original Christian experience, and therefore paradoxically "materialist" – is, historically speaking, also readily identifiable in the Middle Ages, but it was largely on the fringes, at least on the level of critical consciousness and overt statement, up until times extremely close to our own. In any case, within this mindset and way of life, women played a fundamental role, even if the importance of their contribution was too often disregarded or, as nowadays, interpreted in a controversial manner.

In some cases they were conscious of the cultural range of their experience; in others not.

Hildegard von Bingen and Christine de Pizan, for example, demonstrate, in different ways, a complete awareness of the fact that femininity had a particular value within the Christian vision of the medieval world. Hildegard, by exalting the value of art (music primarily), defended herself against the arrogance of the canons of Mainz, who wished to silence her. She showed that women's chant did not hide within itself the deceit of the seductress, but a form of beauty which led to God; or she preached against the Cathars, who negated the value of matter, and even found surprising words to speak with regard to the sexual relationship between a man and a woman. Moreover, in her works dealing with "physics," she highlighted the strength and vitality (*viriditas*) of the created being, whose splendour reflected the colour green, like the branches that revive after a freezing winter. And green was the preferred colour of medieval youth, together with delicate blue, favoured in the fashion of the fourteenth century.

Two centuries after Hildegard, Christine defended the dignity of women in her books (especially *The City of Women*, but not only there), bringing to light a problematic and ongoing element: the female body has a value not to be despised out of an exaggerated asceticism, nor exchanged as a consumer good by false advocates of superficial pleasures. It is in this way that one can understand Christine's heated debate with Jean de Meun and the *Roman de la Rose*.

This position, albeit with nuances of differences due to places, times, and roles, is common to many other women who did not formulate it on the theoretical level, but who did implement it in their day-to-day reality. The transmission of values is not only an intellectual issue.

In each and every case, the medieval women cited in the sixteen stories we have narrated share a common approach, which is presented as a truly effective alternative to a dichotomy that, in part, did exist, but that is often exaggerated in critical circles as the only possible way to represent two faces of the Middle Ages: the goliards (proponents of carnal pleasures), on one side, and the misogynist ascetics, on the other.

These two extreme positions are often evoked, in school manuals, through the juxtaposition of two medieval musical pieces: the *Carmina Burana* and the *Dies Irae*, the first representing the joys of life and the second, in contrast, contempt for the world. These things are true. These things happened and have been documented: but is this all the Middle Ages represents? Do the sixteen stories narrated here seem to fall exclusively within this narrow framework?

Let us ask Agnesina and her impoverished lover, who neither had the money to rowdily sing in taverns nor scorn marriage, but who were helped to marry by a confraternity of laypersons, a charitable organization that almost two thousand women joined. Or let us ask Gigliola, who loved fashion without any qualms, just as her blue dress and silver buttons demonstrated to us. Or we could interrogate Margherita, intent on curing the "flesh" of her sick husband, and thus earning her mother-in-law's praise. Or we could ask Detesalva, Grazia, and Belfiore, who commissioned works of art. But let us pose the question to Bettina, who busied herself with absurd potions in order to help women who wanted to conceive – in other words, nurture the birth of a body.

The body, femininity, beauty.

All of this is part of a historic legacy, to whose transmission medieval women have positively contributed. And in this operation of transmission, these women found not only enemies, but also some allies, among the men they associated with in their lives.

We should remember secretary Volmar in Hildegard's life, or Peter the Venerable in Heloise's, or the husbands of Raingarde and Ottebona, or Francis for Clare and Jacopa, or Christine's great friend, Jean Gerson, or Bridget's followers, and so many others who have loved women.

To all of them, by way of the three men cited in my dedication, I offer up this book, in grateful homage, for their alliance, today urgently in need of renewal.

Stories of Women in the Middle Ages

SOURCES AND BIBLIOGRAPHY

PART ONE: FAMOUS WOMEN

Hildegard, the Genius

On the figure of Hildegard, I refer you, above all, to Peter Dronke, *Women Writers of the Middle Ages: A Critical Study of Texts from Perpetua to Marguerite Porete* (Cambridge: Cambridge University Press, 1984). The same author edited the edition of "Ordo Virtutum" in *Nine Medieval Latin Plays*, edited by Peter Dronke (Cambridge: Cambridge University Press, 1994). On the works of Hildegard, edited and translated into Italian, see: *Cause e cure delle infermità*, edited by Paola Calef (Palermo, Italy: Sellerio, 1997); *"Scivias". Il nuovo cielo e la nuova terra*, edited by Giovanna della Croce (Vatican City: Libreria Editrice Vaticana, 2002); and *Il libro delle opere divine*, edited by Marta Cristiani and Michela Pereira (Milan, Italy: Mondadori, 2003), which has an ample introduction and bibliography. For the principal critical editions of Hildegard's texts, it is essential to consult: *Beate Hildegardis Cause et cure*, edited by Laurence Moulinier, in the series "Rarissima mediaevalia," no. 1 (Berlin: Akademie Verlag, 2003); *Hildegardis Bingensis Epistolarium. Pars prima*: I–XC, edited by Lieven Van Acker (CChr. CM 91) (Turnhout, Belgium: Brepols, 1991); *Hildegardis Bingensis Epistolarium. Pars secunda*: XCI–CCLr, edited by Lieven Van Acker (CChr. CM 91A) (Turnhout, Belgium: Brepols, 1993); *Hildegardis Bingensis Epistolarium. Pars tertia*: CCLI–CCCXC, edited by Lieven Van Acker (†) and Monika Klaes-Hachmöller (CChr. CM 91B) (Turnhout, Belgium: Brepols, 2001); *Hildegardis Bingensis Liber divinorum operum*, edited by Albert Derolez and Peter Dronke (CChr. CM 92) (Turnhout, Belgium: Brepols, 1996); *Hildegardis Bingensis Liber vite meritorum*, edited by Angela Carlevaris (CChr. CM 90) (Turnhout, Belgium: Brepols, 1995); *Vita sanctae Hildegardis*, edited by Monika Klaes (CChr. CM 126) (Turnhout, Belgium: Brepols, 1993); and *Hildegardis Scivias*, edited by Adelgundis Führkotter (CCCM 43) (Turnhout, Belgium: Brepols, 1978). Among the numerous studies on the education of Hildegard, to be recommended is the recent innovative interpretation by Marco Rainini, *Ildegarda, l'eredità di Giovanni Scoto e Hirsau. "Homo medietas" e mediazioni*, in *"Unversehrt und un verletzt." Hildegards von Bingen Menschenbild und Kirchenverständnis heute*, edited by Rainer Berndt, 139–65 (Münster, Germany: Aschendorff, 2015). In order to frame Hildegard within the context of medieval female mysticism, see the beautiful volume *Scrittrici mistiche europee. Secoli XII–XIII*, texts and translations edited by Alessandra Bartolomei Romagnoli, Antonella Degl'Innocenti, and Francesco Santi (Florence, Italy: Edizioni del Galluzzo per la fondazione Ezio Franceschini, 2015). Finally, in terms of the musical works of the Rhenish Abbess (including the two songs I have cited), one should listen to the CD *Ave generosa*, with pieces performed by the choir of the Benedictine Monastery of St Hildegard von Bingen (Musical series Spirto Gentil, 2007, Cooperativa editoriale Nuovo Mondo, distributed by Universal Music).

Raingarde, the Mother

On Raingarde of Montboissier, only one study has appeared in the Italian language, by Paolo Lamma, "La madre di Pietro il Venerabile," in *Studium* 54 (1958): 740–51. Raingarde's biography is based on the *epistola* written by her son and published as number 53 in the following collection: Giles Constable, ed., *The Letters of Peter the Venerable: Champion of Cluny*, Harvard Historical Studies series, no. LXXVIII, I–II (Cambridge, MA, and London: Harvard University Press and Oxford University Press, 1967). Fundamental, in the evaluation of the historical nucleus present in the long *narratio* of this *epistola*, is the study by Peter von Moos, *"Consolatio,"* Studien zur mittelalterlichen Trostliteratur über den Tod und zum Problem der christlichen Trauer, 4 vols. ("Münstersche Mittelalterschriften," III, 1–4) (Munich, Germany: Fink, 1971–72). On the figure of Peter the Venerable considered as an emblem of *discretio* and tolerance, please see: Jean Leclercq, *Pierre le Vénérable* (Abbaye Saint Wandrille, France: Éditions de Fontenelle, 1946); Pietro Zerbi, *Tra Milano e Cluny: momenti di vita e cultura ecclesiastica nel secolo XII* (Rome: Herder, 1978); Jean Pierre Torrell and Denise Bouthillier, *Pierre le Vénérable et sa vision du monde. Sa vie–son œuvre, l'homme et le démon* (Louvain,

Belgium: Spicilegium sacrum lovaniense, 1986); and Maria Teresa Brolis, "La crociata per Pietro il Venerabile: guerra di armi o guerra di idee?" in *Aevum* LXI (1987): 327–54. A different image emerges in another area of study, too influenced, to my mind, by the almost exclusive attention placed on the apologetic works as compared to the other writings of Peter of Cluny; compare Dominique Iogna Prat, *Ordonner et exclure: Cluny et la société chrétienne face à l'hérésie, au judaïsme et à l'islam, 1000–1500* (Paris: Aubier, 1998).

Heloise, the Love–Struck

The seventies and eighties of the last century have been crucial to the progress of studies on the most celebrated couple of medieval lovers. For the letters and the *Historia Calamitatum*, I have based myself on Nada Cappelletti Truci, ed., *Abelardo ed Eloisa. Lettere* (Turin, Italy: Einaudi, 1979). The authenticity of the *Epistolario* between the two of them, after having been questioned by John Benton – see his *Fraud, Fiction, and Borrowing in the Correspondence of Abelard and Heloise,* in *Pierre Abélard – Pierre le Vénérable (Colloque de Cluny, July 1972, Colloques internationaux du CNRS 54),* 469–512 (Paris: CNRS, 1975) – has been recognized (among others) by: Ewald Könsgen, *Epistolae duorum amantium: Briefe Abaelards und Heloises?* (Leiden, Netherlands: Brill, 1974); Pietro Zerbi, "Abelardo ed Eloisa: il problema di un amore e di una corrispondenza," in *Love and Marriage in the Twelfth Century,* edited by Willy Van Hoecke and Andries Welkenhuysen, 130–61 (Louvain, Belgium: Leuven University Press, 1981); Maria Teresa Fumagalli Beonio Brocchieri, *Eloisa e Abelardo* (Milan, Italy: Mondadori, 1984), in particular 216–18; Dronke, *Women Writers of the Middle Ages,* cit., 150–94; and Constant J. Mews, *The Lost Love Letters of Heloise and Abelard: Perceptions of Dialogue in Twelfth Century France* (New York: St Martin's, 1999). For the cultural context, in reference to the theme of marriage, there is an excellent analysis by Jean Leclercq, *I monaci e il matrimonio. Un'indagine sul XII secolo,* edited by Paolo Vian (Turin, Italy: SEI, 1984). Finally, very different, for the chronological-methodological context, but interesting (above all for a balanced reflection on the delicate, controversial, and often "inflated" theme of gender history), is the volume of Didier Lett, *Uomini e donne nel Medioevo. Storia del genere (secoli XII–XV)* (Bologna, Italy: Il Mulino, 2014).

Besides the beautiful volume of Régine Pernoud, *Eleanor of Aquitaine* (Paris: Edition Albin Michel, 1965; London: Collins, 1967), I wish to refer you to Jean Markale, *Eleanor of Aquitaine: The Queen of the Troubadours* (Paris: Payot, 1979; Rochester, VT: Inner Traditions Bear and Company, 2007). More recently, the queen of two crowns has been the object of in-depth analysis in the socio-political and cultural context of her time: "Aliénor d'Aquitaine," in *Association 303. Arts, recherches et creations* 81 (2004); and Marcus Graham Bull and Catherine E. Léglu, eds., *The World of Eleanor of Aquitaine: Literature and Society in Southern France between the Eleventh and Thirteenth Centuries* (Woodbridge, UK: The Boydell Press, 2005). A minute biographical reconstruction characterizes the study by Ralph Vernon Turner, *Eleanor of Aquitaine: Queen of France, Queen of England* (New Haven, CT, and London: Yale University Press, 2009).

Clare, the Founder

For the writings, the biographies, and the Acts of the Process of Canonization of Clare of Assisi (and Francis), I have used the *Fonti Francescane*, Nes edition, edited by Ernesto Caroli (Padua, Italy: Editrici Francescane, 2004). Within the very vast historiography of Clare, I recall only, as works in their entirety: Marco Bartoli, *Chiara d'Assisi* (Rome: Istituto Storico dei Cappuccini, 1989); Marco Bartoli, *Chiara. Una donna tra silenzio e memoria* (Cinisello Balsamo, Edizioni San Paolo, 2001); Chiara Frugoni, *Una solitudine abitata. Chiara d'Assisi* (Roma-Bari, Italy: Laterza, 2006); and let us not forget the beautiful chapter dedicated to Clare by Franco Cardini, in *Francesco d'Assisi*, 143–78 (Milan, Italy: Mondadori, 1989). On Clare's relationship with the pontiffs, it is essential to refer to Maria Pia Alberzoni, *Chiara e il papato* (Milan, Italy: Biblioteca Francescana, 1995). For the development of the Order of the Poor Clares, see Giancarlo Andenna, ed., *Chiara e la diffusione delle Clarisse nel secolo XIII. Atti del Convegno di studi in occasione dell'VIII centenario della nascita di Santa Chiara, Manduria, 14–15 December 1994* (Galatina, Italy: Congedo, 1998). Finally I recommend the proceedings of these two conferences: *Chiara d'Assisi e la memoria di Francesco. Atti del Convegno per l'VIII centenario della nascita di Santa Chiara, Fara Sabina, 19–20 maggio 1994*, edited by Alfonso Marini (Città di Castello, Italy: Petruzzi, 1995); and *Francesco e Chiara d'Assisi: percorsi di ricerca sulle fonti. Atti delle Giornate di Studio. Edizioni e Traduzioni* (Milan, Italy: Università Cattolica del Sacro Cuore, 28 October 2011; Rome: Pontificia Università Antonianum, 9 March 2012; Padua, Italy: EFR, 2014).

Bridget, the Pilgrim

The works dictated by Bridget to her secretaries (*Revelationes e Revelationes extravagantes*) are now easily available at http://www.umilta.net/birgitta.html, without forgetting, obviously, the following critical edition (with English translation): *The Revelations of St. Birgitta of Sweden*, 4 vols., translated by Denis Searby, with an introduction and notes edited by Bridget Morris (Oxford, UK: Oxford University Press, 2006). On the voyages of Bridget see: Sabino de Sandoli, *Viaggio di santa Brigida di Svezia da Roma a Gerusalemme, 1372* (Jerusalem: Franciscan Printing Press, 1991); and Margherita Giordano Lokrantz, "Intorno al viaggio italiano di Birgitta di Svezia: Il soggiorno milanese (autunno 1349)," in *Vestigia. Studi in onore di Giuseppe Billanovich*, edited by Rino Avesani, Mirella Ferrari, Tino Toffano, Giuseppe Frasso, and Agostino Sottili, 387–98 (Rome: Edizioni di Storia e Letteratura, 1984). A collection of the most recent bibliographies, with interesting observations on the relationship between Bridget's spirituality and late medieval iconographic models, can be found in the commendable work by a young scholar, Angela La Delfa, "Le rivelazioni di santa Brigida e l'iconografia. Uno studio dei rapporti tra letteratura spirituale e produzione artistica nel Tardo Medioevo: il caso dei fratelli van Eyck" (Rome: Pontificia Università Gregoriana, doctoral research thesis, 2014–15). Finally I would like to highlight the latest observations by Antonella Degl'Innocenti on the comparison between the *Vita di Brigida* written by Birgero, archbishop of Uppsala, and one written by the Brigidine monk Bertoldo da Roma in the fifteenth century; this reading is recommended to better understand the value of the marital dimension within Bridget's spirituality (appreciated in the first text and devalued in the second): see Antonella Degl'Innocenti, *Spose e madri nell'agiografia medievale, in Religione domestica (medioevo-età moderna)*, in the series Quaderni di storia religiosa, no. 8 (Verona, Italy: Cierre, 2001), 9–53, in particular 30–2. In terms of my initial suggestion to connect Bridget's "historical" life and Kristin's "literary" life to better understand some of Bridget's most human aspects and that of the Nordic context in that period, see Sigrid Undset, *Kristin Lavransdotter*, translated by Tiina Nunnally (New York: Penguin, 1997). And lastly, for the consistency between some Brigidine expressions and those of Charles Péguy, see *Le mystère de la charité de Jeanne d'Arc* (Paris: Gallimard, 1975).

Christine, the Writer

In Italy, the interest in Christine de Pizan was revived towards the end of the nineties of the last century, most especially due to the book *Christine de Pizan. La città delle dame*, edited by Patrizia Caraffi and Earl Jeffrey Richards (Milano-Trento, Italy: Luni Editrice, 1997), from which the citations used in the Italian version of this book come; it was later expanded in Patrizia Caraffi, *Christine de Pizan. La città delle dame* (Rome: Carocci, 2014), although we must not undervalue the previous work of Régine Pernoud, *Storia di una scrittrice medievale. Cristina da Pizzano* (Paris: Calmann-Lévy, 1982; Milan, Italy: Jaca Book, 1996). We also owe to Caraffi a recent edition of a short poem by Christine – *Christine de Pizan. A Giovanna d'Arco* (Florence, Italy: Le Lettere, 2013) – as well as her essay on her relationship with Boccaccio – Patrizia Caraffi, "Boccaccio e Christine de Pizan," in *Boccaccio e i suoi lettori. Una lunga ricezione*, edited by Gian Mario Anselmi, Giovanni Baffetti, Carlo Del Corno, and Sebastiano Nobili, 117–28 (Bologna, Italy: Il Mulino, 2013). Another scholar passionate about Christine is Maria Giuseppina Muzzarelli, *Un'italiana alla corte di Francia. Christine de Pizan, intellettuale e donna* (Bologna, Italy: Il Mulino, 2007), to whom we are also indebted for "Christine di Pizan 'operaia' della ricostruzione storica? Osservazioni intorno al suo 'La vita e i buoni costumi del saggio re Carlo V,'" in *Scritti di storia medievale offerti a Maria Consiglia De Matteis*, edited by Bernardo Pio, 493–513 (Spoleto, Italy: Fondazione Centro Italiano di Studi sull'Alto Medioevo, 2011). With respect to the context of medieval thought with which to compare some statements of Christine, compare Marie-Thérèse d'Alverny, "Le opinioni dei teologi e dei filosofi sulla donna," in *Né Eva né*

Maria. Condizione femminile e immagine della donna nel Medioevo, edited by Michela Pereira, 122–34 (Poitiers, France: 1977; Bologna, Italy: Zanichelli, 1981); while, to my knowledge, there is still missing a study on the relationship between Christine and the *Devotio moderna* (the Modern Devotion reform movement).

On Christine's activity as an "entrepreneur" in the illuminated manuscript sector, see the splendid volume of Gilbert Ouy, Christine Reno, and Inès Villela-Petit, *Album Christine de Pizan*, in the series Texte, Codex & Contexte, no. 14 (Turnhout, Belgium: Brepols, 2012). Lastly we wish to highlight the international conference held in Bologna in 2009 on the overall picture of this extraordinary intellectual: Patrizia Caraffi, ed., *Christine de Pizan. La scrittrice e la città. L'écrivaine et la ville. The Woman Writer and the City* (Florence, Italy: Alinea Editore, 2013). For foreign additions of her other writings, see: Jean-François Kosta-Théfaine, ed., *Christine de Pizan, Une epistre a Eustace Morel, manuscrit Londres, British Library, Harley 4431* ("L'encyclopédie médiévale") (Clermont-Ferrand, France: Paleo, 2010); Christine de Pizan, *Une epistre a la roÿne de France* (manuscript B.N.F. fr. 580) *suive de La lamentacion Cristine de Pizan* (manuscript B.N.F. fr. 24864), edited by Jean-François Kosta-Théfaine (Clermont-Ferrand, France: Paleo, 2010); and Andrea Valentini, ed., *Christine de Pizan, Le livre des epistres du debat sus le "Rommant de la Rose,"* in the series Textes littéraires du Moyen Âge, no. 29 (Paris: Classiques Garnier, 2014). We also recommend consulting the following site for verification of additional bibliographical updates: http://www.arlima.net/ad/ christine_de_pizan.html#.

Joan, the Rebel

The main source upon which I have based my historical reconstruction is the Trial of Condemnation against Joan of Arc, Rouen 1431, edited and translated into Italian by Teresa Cremisi, *Il processo di condanna di Giovanna d'Arco* (Parma, Italy: Guanda, 1977; Milan, Italy: SE, 2000). The vast bibliography on the Maid of Orleans is astutely examined in the best biography about her which we can still read today, thanks to Franco Cardini, *Giovanna d'Arco. La Vergine guerriera* (Milan, Italy: Mondadori, 1998), to which I refer you for additional information.

Out of the eight stories dealt with in the second part, five were launched from the wills of various women; they are those of Flora de Cumis, Ottebona Uliveni, Gigliola Suardi, Femminina de Vazzio (for Margherita de Pillis), and Belfiore da Gorlago. Stored in the archive of the Misericordia Maggiore in Bergamo's Biblioteca Civica Angelo Mai, these last wills and testaments have now been published in Maria Teresa Brolis and Andrea Zonca, *Testamenti di donne a Bergamo nel medioevo*, with a foreword by Attilio Bartoli Langeli (SelciLama [Perugia], Italy: Pliniana, 2012), and are respectively found on pp. 65–9, 20–3, 36–7, 158–61, and 111–13. For further reference to many of the women found in the text, there is another volume often consulted: *La matricola femminile della Misericordia di Bergamo (1265–1339)*, edited by Maria Teresa Brolis, Giovanni Brembilla, and Micaela Corato, with the collaboration of Attilio Bartoli Langeli, in the series Sources et documents d'histoire du Moyen âge, no. 4 (Rome: École française de Rome, 2001).

Flora and Business

On the history of Flora and the other "Bergamasque entrepreneurs" (with additional bibliography and cross-reference to the sources), see my *Ceci in pentola e desiderio di Dio. Religiosità femminile in testamenti bergamaschi (secoli XIII e XIV)*, in *Margini di libertà. Testamenti femminili nel medioevo*, edited by Maria Clara Rossi, 333–55 (Verona, Italy: Cierre, 2010). For the Bergamasque socioeconomic context in this period, see Patrizia Mainoni, "L'economia di Bergamo tra XIII e XV secolo," in *Storia economica e sociale di Bergamo. I primi Millenni. Il Comune e la Signoria*, 257–305 (Bergamo, Italy: Bolis, 1999). I would like to thank Patrizia Mainoni for the archival recommendation relating to the merchant Ottabona of Desenzano (Archivio di Stato di Bergamo, Fondo Notarile, notary Pecino da Gaverina, in the year 1365).

The dowry of Fantina Polo is transcribed in *Donne di Venezia. Mostra documentaria*, edited by Alessandro Schiavon and Chiara Scarpa, 45–51 (Venice, Italy: Archivio di Stato di Venezia, 2012). For the story of Maria, wife of the doge Pietro Ziani, see Fernanda Sorelli, "Diritto, economia, società: condizioni delle donne a Venezia nei secoli XII–XIII," in *Donne, lavoro,* economia a Venezia e in Terraferma tra Medioevo ed età moderna, edited by Anna Bellavitis and Linda Guzzetti, 19–40, especially 24, in "Archivio Veneto," VI, 3 (2012). For Giacoma, active in business in Bari around 1224, see Patrizia Mainoni, "A proposito di fiducia: mogli, tutrici ed 'epitropisse' nei testamenti pugliesi (secoli XIII–XIV)," in *Dare credito alle donne. Presenze femminili nell'economia tra medioevo ed età moderna*, edited by Giovanna Petti Balbi and Paola Guglielmotti, 89 (Asti, Italy: Centro studi Renato Bordone sui lombardi, sul credito e sulla banca, 2012). I refer you also to other essays in this latter important volume, and in particular that of Angela Orlandi, "Le merciaie di Palma. Il commercio dei veli nella Maiorca di fine Trecento," 149–66.

On female entrepreneurship in the world of work, see Maria Giuseppina Muzzarelli, *Un'introduzione alla storiografia*, in *Donne e lavoro nell'Italia medievale*, edited by Maria Giuseppina Muzzarelli, Paola Galetti, and Bruno Andreolli (Turin, Italy: Rosenberg & Sellier, 1991); to be compared (extending consideration to the broader theme of the historiography on medieval women) with Enrica Guerra, *Donne medievali. Un percorso storico e metodologico* (Ferrara, Italy: Edizioni Nuovecarte, 2006); but also with Patricia Skinner, *Le donne nell'Italia medievale* (Rome: Viella, 2005); and Tiziana Lazzari, *Le donne nell'alto Medioevo* (Turin and Milan, Italy: Pearson Italia-Mondadori, 2010). Though older, an important reference remains lastly that of Georges Duby and Michelle Perrot, *Storia delle donne in Occidente. II. Il Medioevo*, edited by Christiane Klapisch-Zuber (Roma-Bari: Laterza, 1990).

Agnesina and Poverty

The dowry of Agnesina Baroni is conserved in the Biblioteca Civica Angelo Mai of Bergamo, in the archive of the Misericordia Maggiore (MIA, ms. 1245, f. 94r). In terms of Agnesina and other poor women of Bergamo, allow me to refer to my own *Le opere della MIA. L'assistenza*, in *Collana per il 7500 anno di fondazione della Congregazione della Misericordia Maggiore di Bergamo*, vol. VI, edited by Attilio Bartoli Langeli, 5–38 (Bergamo, Italy: Bolis, 2015), as well as the lists of the poor, published in the often-cited *Matricola femminile* of the MIA Foundation. Other sources on the poor aided by the Misericordia Maggiore are highlighted in Roisin Cossar, *The Transformation of Laity in Bergamo, 1265–c.1400* (Boston: Brill, 2006).

On the topic of poverty in the Middle Ages, the reference to Michel Mollat, *I poveri nel Medioevo* (Roma-Bari: Laterza, 1983), still remains fundamental. To this we can add these subsequent studies: Enrico Menestò, ed., *La conversione alla povertà nell'Italia dei secoli XII–XIV (Todi, 14–17 October 1990)* (Spoleto, Italy: CISAM, 1991); Vera Zamagni, ed., *Povertà e innovazioni istituzionali in Italia. Dal Medioevo ad oggi* (Bologna, Italy: Il Mulino, 2000); and Giuliana Albini, *Carità e governo delle povertà (secoli XIIXV)* (Milan, Italy: Unicopli, 2002).

Ottebona and Marriage

Medieval marriage is in possession of a very ample literature. Although not new, the synthesis by David Herlihy, *La famiglia nel medioevo* (Boston: Harvard University Press, 1985; Roma-Bari: Laterza, 1987) is still important. With respect to the evolution of lineage towards the marital unit, I wish merely to recall Cinzio Violante, *Alcune caratteristiche delle strutture familiari in Lombardia, Emilia e Toscana durante i secoli IX–XII*, in *Famiglia e parentela nell'Italia medievale*, edited by Georges Duby and Jacques Le Goff, 19–82 (Rome: 1977; Bologna, Italy: Il Mulino, 1981), and Georges Duby, *Medioevo maschio. Amore e matrimonio* (Roma-Bari: Laterza, 2002), in particular 122–3.

In terms of the relationship between medieval theology and the value of marriage, besides the already-mentioned Leclercq, *I monaci e il matrimonio*, cited, I refer to the considerations (cited verbatim by myself in the text) drawn from Jacques Le Goff, *Il cielo sceso in terra. Le radici medievali dell'Europa* (Roma-Bari: Laterza, 2009), 101–2.

On the legal limitations attributed, with regional variants, to women's ability to act in late medieval Italy, see Manlio Bellomo, *Ricerche sui rapporti patrimoniali tra coniugi. Contributo alla storia della famiglia medievale* (Milan, Italy: Giuffrè, 1961); Andrea Romano, *Famiglia, successioni e patrimonio familiare nell'Italia medievale e moderna* (Turin, Italy: Giappichelli, 1994); Maria Teresa Guerra Medici, *L'aria di città. Donne e diritti nel comune medievale* (Naples, Italy: ESI, 1996); and Giulia Calvi and Isabelle Chabot, eds., *Le ricchezze delle donne. Diritti patrimoniali e poteri familiari in Italia (XIII–XIX secc.)* (Turin, Italy: Rosenberg & Sellier, 1998). In this regard, on the legal situation in Bergamo, I refer to Brolis-Zonca, *Testamenti di donne*, cited, in particular xxiii–xxxi.

Grazia d'Arzago and her reform work have been studied by Mariarosa Cortesi, *Il Legendario di Santa Grata: Tra scrittura agiografica e arte*, in collaboration with Giordana Mariani Canova (Bergamo, Italy: Istituto Grafico Litostampa, 2002); and by Giovanni Brembilla, "Il monastero di Santa Grata in Bergamo: contributi per una storia istituzionale e per una ricostruzione del patrimonio fondiario (secoli XII–XIII)," in *Bergomum* 79 (2005): 14–23. On Abbess Berlenda da Urgnano, we have Paolo Nobili, "Storia di un fallimento. Il monastero di San Pietro de Brozate e la colonizzazione di un lembo della bassa bergamasca (secoli XII–XIII)," in *Nuova Rivista Storica* 95 (2011): 1005–24; on the other small Bergamasque female convents, see my essay "Un monastero assalito dagli uomini, ignorato dagli storici e ricostruito dalle monache. S. Maria di Valmarina presso Bergamo (secoli XII–XV)," in *Chiesa, vita religiosa, società nel Medioevo italiano. Studi offerti a Giuseppina De Sandre Gasparini*, edited by Mariaclara Rossi and Gian Maria Varanini, 121–37 (Rome: Herder, 2005). For the female Humiliati and Augustinians of Redona, I must again refer to two of my studies, respectively: *Gli Umiliati a Bergamo nei secoli XIII–XIV* (Milan, Italy: Vita e Pensiero, 1991); and "Il governo femminile nelle comunità doppie: S. Giorgio di Redona, in Uomini e donne in comunità," in *Quaderni di storia religiosa* 1 (1994): 177–87. There does not exist, however, an overall study on women's eremitic experiences in the Bergamo area; the cases cited have emerged from the published lists in the Female Register of the Misericordia Maggiore.

On female monasticism in medieval Italy, together with the review edited by Annalisa Albuzzi, "Il monachesimo femminile nell'Italia medioevale. Spunti di riflessione e prospettive di ricerca in margine alla produzione storiografica degli ultimi trent'anni," in *Dove va la storiografia monastica in Europa? Temi e metodi di ricerca per lo studio della vita monastica e regolare in età medievale alle soglie del terzo millennio. Atti del Convegno internazionale (Brescia-Rodengo 23–25 marzo 2000)*, 131–89 (Milan, Italy: Vita e Pensiero, 2001), and with the reflections of Vincenza Musardo Salò, "Per una fenomenologia del monachesimo femminile medievale," in *Communio* 198 (2004): 44–51, I recommend the following volumes taken together, and, most recently, an excellent study on the local level (I also refer you to these texts for further bibliographic references): Gabriella Zarri, ed., *Il monach-esimo femminile in Italia dall'alto medioevo al secolo XVII. A confronto con l'oggi. Atti del VI Convegno del "Centro di Studi Farfensi," Santa Vittoria in Mantenano, 21–24 settembre 1995* (San Pietro in Cariano, Italy: Il Segno dei Gabrielli, 1997); Jo Ann Kay McNamara, *Sisters in Arms: Catholic Nuns through Two Millennia* (Cambridge, MA: Harvard University Press, 1998); and Silvia Carraro, *La laguna delle donne. Il monachesimo femminile a Venezia tra IX e XIV secolo* (Pisa, Italy: Pisa University Press, 2015).

For other forms of religious life, I restrict myself to one classic: Herbert Grundmann, *Movimenti religiosi nel Medioevo. Ricerche sui nessi storici tra l'eresia, gli Ordini mendicanti e il movimento religioso femminile nel XII e XIII secolo e sui presupposti storici della mistica tedesca* (Bologna, Italy: Il Mulino, 1974). In reference to Italy (with particular attention to the recluses), see Anna Benvenuti, *"In castro penitenciae." Santità e società femminile nell'Italia medievale* (Rome: Herder, 1990); and, within the larger context of female sanctity, we should not forget André Vauchez, *La santità nel Medioevo* (Bologna, Italy: Il Mulino, 1989).

Gigliola and Fashion

For the most important studies on fashion in the thirteenth and fourteenth centuries, see: Rosita Levi-Pisetzky, *Storia del costume in Italia*, vols. II–III (Milan, Italy: Istituto dell'Enciclopedia Italiana, 1964–66); *La voce Abbigliamento. L'Occidente*, edited by Françoise Piponnier, in *Enciclopedia dell'Arte Medievale* (1991); Michel Pastoureau, *Blu. Storia di un colore* (Milan, Italy: Ponte alle Grazie, 2002); and Maria Giuseppina Muzzarelli, *Guardaroba medievale. Vesti e società dal XIII al XVI secolo* (Bologna, Italy: Il Mulino, 2008).

Bettina and Her Potions

The trial of Bettina da Gandino was published by the person who wrote "Donne e assistenza a Bergamo nei secoli XIII e XIV: benefattrici, assistite e forme di marginalità femminile," in *Nuova Rivista Storica* 85 (2001): 619–50, in particular 648–50. An updated study on medieval heresy is lacking for Bergamo. For this reason, we still have to resort to Gerolamo Biscaro,

"Inquisitori ed eretici lombardi (1292–1318)," in *Miscellanea di storia italiana* III, no. 19 (1922): 445–557; Angelo Mazzi, "Aspetti di vita religiosa e civile nel secolo XIII a Bergamo," in *Bollettino della Civica Biblioteca di Bergamo* 16 (1922): 189–277; and Christine Thouzellier, "Polémique sur l'origine de l'hérésie à Bergame aux XIIe–XIIIe s.," in *Revue d'histoire ecclésiastique* 62 (1967): 421–8 (this last one is available online at http://www.mgh-bibliothek.de//etc/dokumente/a102801.pdf). More recently the theme has been reprised by Angelita Roncelli in her doctoral thesis: "Chiesa, Comune e frati Predicatori a Bergamo nella prima metà del XIII secolo" (Milan, Italy: Università Cattolica di Milano, 2010–11), 75–87. For the admonitions of Bishop Giovanni da Scanzo against witchcraft practices, see Giovanni Finazzi, ed., *Sinodo diocesano tenuto in Bergamo l'anno 1304 sotto il vescovo Giovanni da Scanzo* (Milan, Italy: Bonardi Pogliani, 1853), 24. Episodes of iconophagia in Bergamo have been reconstructed by Giosuè Bonetti, "Testimonianze figurative della pietà popolare a Bergamo dal medioevo alla controriforma. Per un catalogo delle immagini devozionali" (Milan, Italy: Università Cattolica di Milano, degree thesis, 1984–85), 244, who has kindly recommended to me *gli atti del processo alle donne, sorprese con la polvere da mettere nella minestra dei mariti* (the proceedings of trials against women, caught with putting "scrapings" in the soup of their husbands): Bergamo, Archivio diocesano, *Processi per eresia e superstizioni*, ms. XVI–XVII century, c. 178.

On the broader issue of therapeutic or "magic" practices among women and on the transmission of "medical" knowledge from woman to woman, besides the classic study by Franco Cardini, *Magia, stregoneria, superstizioni nell'Occidente medievale* (Florence, Italy: La Nuova Italia, 1979), I refer you to Marina Montesano, *"Supra acqua et supra ad vento." Superstizioni, maleficia e incantamenta nei predicatori francescani Osservanti (Italia, sec. XV)* (Rome: Istituto storico italiano per il Medioevo, 1999), and Gabriella Piccinni, *La trasmissione dei saperi delle donne*, in *La trasmissione dei saperi nel Medioevo (secoli XII–XV)* (Pistoia, Italy: Centro Italiano di Studi di Storia e d'Arte, 2005), 205–47.

For the problem of the relationship between heresy and women, we have a very interesting hypothesis proposed, in her time, by Eleanor McLaughlin, "Women and Medieval Heresy," in *Concilium*, vol. CXI (1976): 99–114, whose interpretation is different (actually opposite) to that of Gottfried Koch, "La donna nel Catarismo e nel Valdismo medievali," in *Medioevo ereticale*, edited by Ovidio Capitani, 245–76 (Bologna, Italy: Il Mulino, 1983). Also see, for studies on specific areas or for individual cases of heretical women: Jacques Dalarun, *"Lapsus linguae." La légende de Claire de Rimini*, in the series Biblioteca di Medioevo Latino, no. 6 (Spoleto, Italy: CISAM, 1994); Daniela Müller, *Frauen vor der Inquisition. Lebensform, Glaubenszeugnis und Aburteilung der deutschen und französischen Katharerinnen* (Mainz, Germany: Philipp von Zabern, 1996); Marina Benedetti, *Io non sono Dio. Guglielma di Milano e i Figli dello Spirito Santo* (Milan, Italy: Biblioteca Francescana, 2004); and Lorenzo Paolini, "Domina Mirabella de Faventia" (forthcoming in *Rivista di storia della Chiesa in Italia*).

For a recent reflection on the use of the term "heretic" in relation to different historiographic tendencies, see Grado Giovanni Merlo, *Eretici del Medioevo. Temi e paradossi di storia e storiografia* (Brescia, Italy: Morcelliana, 2011); and Jacques Dalarun, "La charte de Niquinta. Débats heuristiques, enjeux herméneutiques," in *Aevum* 86, no. 2 (2012): 535–48.

Margherita and Care-Giving

On various aspects of women's day-to-day lives one cannot exclude *Religione domestica (medioevo-età moderna)*, edited by G. De Sandre Gasparini, in the series Quaderni di storia religiosa, no. 8 (Verona, Italy: Cierre, 2001), in which new horizons open up on the theme of daily life (or normality) that "although constituting the skeleton of the existence of men and women in all periods, it manages, for the most part, to escape the analysis of the historian": Giuseppina De Sandre Gasparini, *Apertura di un tema, in Fedeli in chiesa*, in Quaderni di storia religiosa, no. 6 (Verona, Italy: Cierre, 1999), 15. On the formation of laywomen's religiosity, an important source is the specialized preaching addressing women; on this subject, see: Carla Casagrande, ed., *Prediche alle donne nel secolo XIII* (Milan, Italy: Bompiani, 1978); Laura Restelli, *Parigi 1272: Prediche alle donne* (Rome: Edizioni Associate, 2001); and Sofia Boesch Gajano, ed., *Storia della direzione spirituale. II. L'età medievale* (Brescia, Italy: Morcelliana, 2010). Starting from the early modern era, there are many interesting sources available, such as the letters of teachers and confessors to women, or images of personal devotion; compare Daniela Delcorno Branca, *Il "Giardino novello." Lettere di direzione spirituale del Quattrocento trasmesse dalle monache del Paradiso, in*

del secolo XV," in *Margini di libertà*, cited, 381–404; and Gabriella Zarri,
e famiglie 'allargate' nei testamenti degli uomini e delle donne veronesi
(2005): 177–247; Maria Clara Rossi, "Figli d'anima. Forme di 'adozione'
Murate e la pellegrina Eugenia," in *Archivio italiano per la storia della pietà* 18
103–4; Denise Stocchetti, "La fondazione del monastero fiorentino delle
nesi (sec. XV)," in *Ricerche di storia sociale e religiosa* 64 (2003): 95–116, esp.
Cierre, 2000); Giuseppina De Sandre Gasparini, "Dai testamenti vero-
Pellegrini e vie del pellegrinaggio a Treviso nel Medioevo (sec. XII–XV) (Verona, Italy:
di Storia Patria, 1952), vol. 11, n. 1319. See as well: Giampaolo Cagnin,
edited by H.C. Krueger and R.L. Reynolds (Genoa, Italy: Società Ligure
transport costs: see Lanfranco [1202–26], in *Notai liguri del sec. XII e del XIII*,
tanaria, wife of Martino de Mari the draper, left 100 coins for overseas
is still very interesting, to Valeria Polonio: on 21 December 1216, Mon-
ing story, which I did not insert into this chapter, but which I maintain
Italy: Società Ligure di Storia Patria, 1999), esp. 114–15. I owe the follow-
genovese dalle origini ai nostri giorni, edited by Dino Puncuh, 77–210 (Genoa,
localismo: costruzione di un sistema (569–1321)," in *Il cammino della Chiesa*
della Bibl. Franzoniana, 1994), 29; Valeria Polonio. "Tra universalismo e
internazionale di studi, Genoa, 9–11 December 1993 (Genoa, Italy: Assoc. Amici
in *Gli Agostiniani a Genova e in Liguria tra Medioevo ed età moderna. Atti del Convegno*
Valeria Polonio. *Canonici regolari, istituzioni e religiosità in Liguria (secoli XII–XIII)*,
Rationarium vitae, edited by Vittore Nason (Florence, Italy: Olschki, 1986);
vich (Milan, Italy: Artigianelli, 1900); Giovanni Conversini da Ravenna,
Suriano, *Il Trattato di Terrasanta e dell'Oriente*, edited by Girolamo Golubo-
About the cases of Italian women pilgrims I have cited, see: Francesco

Belfiore on the Road

http://fermi.univr.it/rm/repertorio/rm-gazzini-ospedali-medioevo.
medievale, edited by Marina Gazzini, in "Reti medievali. Repertorio," 2012,
7–40; and for general context, I refer you to the review *Ospedali nell'Italia*
"Ospedali e assistenza a Bergamo nel medioevo," in *Bergomum* 102 (2007):
On the history of hospitals, for the city of Bergamo, see my own
delle immagini (Roma-Bari: Laterza, 2011).
Da Dante a Montale, in onore di Emilio Pasquini (Bologna, Italy: Gedit, 2005),
307–22; and Ottavia Niccoli. *Vedere con gli occhi del cuore. Alle origini del potere*

"Il pellegrinaggio tra Quattro e Cinquecento: Viaggi reali e viaggi immaginari," in *Donne in viaggio, viaggi di donne. Uno sguardo nel lungo periodo*, edited by Rita Mazzei, 43–58 (Florence, Italy: Le Lettere, 2009).

In terms of the general context, compare Anna Benvenuti, "Donne sulla strada: L'itineranza religiosa feminile nel Medioevo," in *Donne in viaggio*, edited by Maria Luisa Silvestre and Adriana Valerio, 74–86 (Roma-Bari: Laterza, 1999); Franco Cardini, *In Terrasanta. Pellegrini italiani tra Medioevo e prima età moderna* (Bologna, Italy: Il Mulino, 2002); Luisa Lofoco, "Le donne alle crociate: Primi appunti," in *Schola Salernitana. Annali* 10 (2005): 209–34; Andrea Rottloff, "*Stärker als Männer und tapferer als Ritter.*" *Pilgerinnen in Spätantike und Mittelalter* (Mainz, Germany): Philipp von Zabern, 2007); and Maria Serena Mazzi, *In viaggio nel Medioevo* (Bologna, Italy: Il Mulino, 2016). Even if it dates back to late Antiquity, one must not forget the story of Egeria, reconstructed so well by Franco Cardini in "Egeria, la pellegrina," in *Medioevo al femminile*, edited by Ferruccio Bertini, 3–30 (Roma-Bari: Laterza, 1989).

IN AN EFFORT NOT TO CONCLUDE ...

About the letter of Francis of Assisi to Jacopa, see Ernesto Caroli, ed., *Fonti Francescane. Nuova edizione* (Padua, Italy: Editrici Francescane, 2004), 158. On Jacopa dei Settesogli, married to Graziano dei Frangipane, there is an entry being drafted now for the *Dizionario Biografico degli Italiani* (the *Biographical Dictionary of Italians*), edited by Alfonso Marini, who dedicates some references to the Roman noblewoman in his *Francesco d'Assisi, il mercante del regno* (Rome: Carocci, 2015) esp. 39–40, 108, 205–7, 211–12, 240; he clarifies, among other things, that it has not been proven that Jacopa comes from the Norman family (a prior hypothesis formulated in 1927 by Édouard d'Alençon) and how it is preferable to render the surname of de Septemsoliis (deriving from the dwellings of that branch of the Frangipane family situated in Settizonio near the Circus Maximus) as "Settesogli" and not as "Settesoli." In terms of her first name, I also share Marini's proposition not to translate it as "Giacoma" but to leave it as "Jacopa." When, in my conclusions, I hinted at a Christian philosophical trend which was "largely on the fringes, at least on the level of critical consciousness and overt statement, up until times extremely close to our own," I was obviously referring to various post-conciliar theologians and papal documents, but I maintain that the most surprising evidence of a radical change in the Christian vision on eros and women has come from the last two pontiffs. See, for instance, the bold assessments expressed about the relationship between eros and agape by Benedict XVI in the encyclical *Deus Caritas est* (Vatican City: Libreria Editrice Vaticana, 2005), 10–23. With respect to Pope Francis, I refer you especially to the chapter *La dimensione erotica dell'amore nell'esortazione apostolica Amoris Letitia* (Rome: Edizioni San Paolo, 2016), paragraphs 150–7. These two texts would be enough to reopen (finally!) the debate on the theme from a decidedly new perspective. And lastly, with regards to the emphasis informing my conclusions on the prevalence of the "Christian mentality" within the "medieval mentalities" (fully recognizing, however, other decisive influences), I refer you to the "Intervista ad André Vauchez" ("Interview with André Vauchez"), edited by Umberto Longo and Gian Maria Varanini, in *Reti Medievali Rivista* 15, no. 1 (2014), http://www.rmojs.unina.it/index.php/rm/article/view File/4856/5446, which is presented as a balanced and complete synthesis on this topic, as well, within the context of a rich *excursus* on medieval studies (not only Italian) in recent decades.